Playground
To
Parade Ground

FAUJI BRAT TO MILITARY SPOUSE

GANIV PANJRATH

THE
CROW'S
LEGACY
PUBLISHERS

Published by

Office: B/22 GF

Vasant Kunj Enclave
New Delhi-110070
Phone- +91 9953758404

Emails:
crowslegacy72@gmail.com

Website: www.thecrowslegacy.com

© **Ganiv Panjrath, 2024**

First Published–2024

ISBN 13: 978-9391526368

ISBN 10: 9391526365

MRP: ₹ 615/-

Book size: 5.5" x8.5"

Printed and bound by Crows Legacy Publishers OPC Pvt. Ltd., New Delhi

Contents

• **Part 3: A Lifetime of Wisdom and Resilience**

Epilude: Army Life "Roles & Reflections"

Mission Gratitude

Dedication

To Kiran, Mahip, and Kuki—my parents, grandparents, and family—who have unfurled the chapters of my life and nurtured my upbringing with unwavering family values.

Sheri and Tannaaz, whom I appreciate, whose consistent encouragement and gentle prods have propelled me toward the world of writing.

Life in the army, first as a "brat" and then as a spouse has been my guiding force, my mentor. It taught me all that I know, the significance of loyalty and integrity, the sense of kinship and camaraderie. Through my book, I would like to shout out to the resolute and unsung partners who stand as unwavering pillars of strength behind their uniformed counterparts.

I'd like to include Kirat, my son, as my most lovable discerning critic and invaluable supporter.

Foreword

Our soldiers are the finest in the world. What makes them so is the intensive training they undergo, the ethos of the organisation they belong to, and an innate sense of duty and purpose both of these instil in each one of them. But there is also a third, lesser-known secret behind their excellence. Every soldier is powered by his or her own private army. It is manned (and womaned) by each member of their family. They are the strength behind the individual in uniform, their inspiration, strength and driving force. Spouses, parents, children, siblings – the unsung heroes and heroines who share the trials and tribulations that the soldiers themselves undergo but rarely come in the limelight. They provide the bedrock of stability and uncomplaining emotional support that enables the soldiers to discharge their duties without concern or care.

'Playground to Parade ground' is an eloquent narration of the first-hand experiences of one such private army. Growing up as a cantonment brat and then marrying into the Army, Ganiv has come across the full spectrum of the roller coaster ride. There is a marked contrast between the two roles. They say it takes a village to raise a child. In the case of a cantonment brat, the entire unit or even the entire garrison pitches in. The carefree existence as an officer's child is one where the world (or at least the military station) is your oyster and you can explore your potential knowing fully well that you have your extended family to back you up. The transition into the responsible role of an officer's wife is a metamorphosis without the cocoon stage per se. You grow up fast and realise that you're on the other side of the fence now, providing the same support that you received from the extended family. The journey has been related in an inimitable witty style that raises more than one chuckle as you go through it. The rib tickling sketches by Capt Anshuman Chatterjee add a visual delight to the narration.

Now that Ganiv has finally taken up the pen herself, her rich experience as a publisher shines through in the crafting of her words and her work. Having stewarded umpteen authors (including myself) towards their publications, Ganiv's own debut as an author is bound to be the spectacular success it deserves to be. Since you're reading this, the book is obviously in your hands. Whether you yourself are a brat, a spouse, or both, you will surely find more than one thread of familiarity with your own experience within the pages. It will make you smile nostalgically, sigh regretfully, and maybe even shed a tear or two. Once you have finished enjoying it, do not forget to do your bit by spreading the word about it, as authors deserve all the encouragement and visibility they can get.

Lt Col Rohit Agarwal (Retd.),

Veteran and Author

Prelude

The idea of authoring a book popped up into my head while I was chomping on a mouthful of pizza. Probably not the most glamorous moment, but hey, inspiration strikes in the most unexpected places. I decided to write in the first person because I wanted the readers to feel like they were right there with me, experiencing everything I had experienced. The real challenge began when I started to write. My initial draft was a complete disaster. My writing was choppy, and the plot was all over the place. It was as if the story had a mind of its own, just like my father used to say when he told his wild tales.

After many sleepless nights and gallons of coffee, I finally had a manuscript which I was happy with. My friends, knowing my penchant for humour, nudged me and asked, if everyone has a story, what about you, carrying on your father's legacy of running Creative Crows? Can the publisher write a book too?" It was a humorous, yet priceless reminder of the creative genes passed down by my dad.

Sheri, (my husband) and my friend Shivaji who took time to help me fill in the blanks, were my redeeming features during the editing process. Patiently guiding me through the maze of revisions. I had to cut down on my endless use of adjectives and adverbs, and my editor had to remind me constantly that not every sentence needs an exclamation mark, just as my father used to guide me through life's challenges with his wisdom and wit.

Once the manuscript was in decent shape, it was time to design the cover. I thought I had this in the bag, but boy, I was mistaken. I had to go through so many versions of the cover Whenever I thought I had finally found the perfect one, another terrific version was be suggested!

Finally, it was time to print the book. I was so eager to see my words on paper, but I was also terrified. What if people didn't like it? What if they thought it was the worst book they'd ever read? But as the books arrived, and I held the first copy in my hand, I knew that all the effort, sweat, and tears had been worth it, just as my father had always said - "Keep going, no matter what."

Overall, the journey of making a book in the first-person account was a hilarious rollercoaster ride. There were so many moments where I just laughed at myself and the absurdity of it all. From pizza to print, the journey was a laughter riot, and I wouldn't have had it any other way. In the end, I realised I was not only drafting a book but also carrying on my father's legacy of creativity and humour, one page at a time.

PART I
LITTLE SOLDIERS AND
FREQUENT MOVERS

In childhood's embrace, as an army man's child,
loved and cared for, in adventures wild.
Travels and separations, woven into our tale,
no regrets linger, memories prevail.

The Golden Years—1976

My journey begins at a remote small town called Poonch in Jammu & Kashmir (J&K), not for any other reason but, for that fun-filled, exciting summer sojourn to the quaint little border town of Pooch. That's because, it is my first definitive memory, …as far as I can remember!

It all began when an inland letter arrived at my maternal grandparents' house in Delhi, addressed to my mum. Even though it was covered in black marks from being censored, just seeing the words 'My love, Gogi' written by my dad, who was serving somewhere in the northern part of our country. It was enough to give my mum her ideal dose of happiness, that would last a whole month. This one time, specifically, her level of excitement had gone through the roof, affecting all those around her including her daughters, us two sisters!

I, Gonu (Ganiv), was the elder of the two siblings, the

younger one being Gini (Jyotan). Our mother, Kiran, (the eldest of three sisters), was a perfect homemaker and our father, Mahip - Col Mahip Chadha - (the eldest of three brothers), was a tall, and charismatic officer of the Indian Army's 3rd Gorkha Rifles. We were a quintessential *'fauji* Family.' Life for a three-year-old meant fun, frolic, momma's unconditional love, and looking forward to meeting one's 'Infantryman' papa. He was our superhero and I remember eagerly waiting to see my dad, who was often away on missions and clamouring to hear all about his adventures in the army.

Gini and I will never forget the jokes and laughter. My father had a deep sense of humour and would keep us in stitches with his jokes. I can still hear him telling us the classic 'Why did the tomato turn red?' joke, followed by a punchline that had us laughing so hard, our sides hurt. If you put your mind to it, you will guess, for the answer is as plain as the nose on your face.

Our trip to Poonch that summer was the first lively, fun-filled family reunion in memory. We had picnics, barbecues, and many outdoor activities arranged for us. I recall having a surreal feeling of living life as in a beautiful film where families gather, have a magical time, and plentiful happily ever-after moments. But that's what growing up in a *'fauji* Family' was like - always filled with excitement and love.

Memories of the family reunion in Poonch will always be treasured, like hidden gems. I can vividly recall the smell of my mother's cooking even today, decades later. As we sat to dine at a six-seater, so I always felt as though we were a big,

big happy, loving family, even though we were just four; without the extended family. The menu we were presented with at that table was truly multicuisine and multicultural. My mother would make dishes inspired by Punjabi cuisine, while my father would bring back recipes from his travels around the country. Flavours from all over the states, Northern, Southern, Eastern, and Western, would come together to be savoured in our home. This is but one example of the way a *fauji* fosters national integration!

And then the letter arrived! This letter was no ordinary one. It was an invitation to mum and us to visit dad in Jammu & Kashmir over the summer break. My mum didn't waste a single moment; we had to pack our bags and get our train reservation sorted (yes, this was before the days of online booking). My grandma (*Naniji*) got busy whipping up delicious meals for us to enjoy on the train, and she packed enough goodies to keep us satiated for the long overnight journey to Jammu.

It was a scene straight out of a classic family movie. Those must have been days filled with bliss if, occasionally, I imagined I was living a scene from a film! The hustle and bustle of packing, the sound and aromas of my grandma's kitchen, and the excitement of visiting my dad were too much for my young mind to handle. And to think that all this frenzy had resulted from a simple letter. So very *'filmi'*—where a letter from far away is a symbol of hope and adventure.

Who knows, maybe one day I'll tell my little brood about this exciting journey and the power of a simple letter, which had been written in a small bunker admeasuring 3 feet by 3 feet and overlooking the enemy target.

As a young girl, I always longed for adventures; and the trip to Poonch was a dream come true in that context. We set off for the railway station from our maternal grandparents' house in Delhi in my grandfather's (*Nanaji's*) vintage 1960s FIAT, with my grandfather (*Nanaji*) sporting a cushion for his backache, we girls found this quite funny. Despite the lack of air conditioning (unheard of those days), the three of us were thrilled to be travelling First Class in an exclusive coupe.

Mummy was always the voice of caution, reminding us not to leave her hand, to follow the '*coolie*' (a porter dressed in a red *kurta* and white *dhoti*) assisting us in carrying our suitcases, not to go to the lavatory alone at night, and not to open the windows. But all her instructions were forgotten as we chatted non-stop with the ticket-checking 'uncle,' popularly known as the TTE, whom we quickly filled up on our exciting journey to meet our 'Infantryman' father in Poonch.

The train ride was the highlight of the journey. Despite convenient and affordable air travel today, nothing is as soul-satisfying as a train journey. The clickety clacking harmonious melody of carriages on the tracks, picturesque hamlets, noisy platforms with energetic vendors—each one boasting its local fare, pastures, swaying crops, the simple joy of a train journey remains unmatched.

Just as the engine jolted to life and the lights in the coupe came on, I couldn't help but feel a rush of excitement. We were off, and I was in a state of anticipation of something, yet not known to me.

As the train made its way through the countryside, Nani's delicious *parathas* (wheat bread rolled flat and baked) and *aloo matar sabzi* (vegetables) and potato with *aam ka achaar* (mango pickle) filled our compartment with the warm and comforting aroma of home-cooked food. I cannot help but wonder that no matter how many times I've had this meal at home, that distinct delicious taste still lingers in memory. It always tasted extra special when we were travelling.

After a satisfying meal, it was time for bed. Mummy took out her trusty pillow cover and hid her valuables inside, ensuring that her precious belongings were safe and secure. With the lights switched off, she made sure to double-check the door, just the way my dad would check the perimeter before settling in for the night. It was a familiar routine and one that brought comfort amidst the excitement of our travels.

As I drifted off to sleep. I couldn't help but chuckle at the thought of how different my bedtime routine was compared to my friends back in Delhi. But despite the differences, one thing was for sure—a good night's sleep, was essential for any journey, whether it was a trip to Poonch or an adventure around the world—something I were to experience much later in life on turbulent, long trans-oceanic flights.

As the sound of the vendor shouting, *'Chai Chai!'* (Tea-Tea) filled the air, we knew that our long journey was finally ending. Waking up to the call for tea in the enigmatically piercing tone of the tea vendor, accompanied by his special brand of clanging, is truly a feeling that cannot be replicated no matter how luxuriously you may travel elsewhere in the world.

I hugged myself, ecstatic at the thought of getting closer to papa, as the train pulled into Jammu Tawi station. We were now just two days away from meeting him. The excitement was palpable, with our mother trying her best to contain her smile as we excitedly chattered away about finally seeing papa after so many months.

We stepped off the train and made our way to the transit bus that was waiting to take us to the Transit Camp in Jammu. It was a welcome change from the long train journey, and we were thrilled to explore this new place. We knew we would spend the night there before taking another bus through the winding, scenic mountain tracks of Akhnoor Hills to Narian Camp.

After two days of travelling and a night spent on the train, we finally arrived at Narian Camp. On the third day, after an exhausting but exhilarating journey of three days and two nights, we were about to reach our destination. I was sure that we would make some cherished and unforgettable memories.

It was disappointing that when we finally arrived, papa was nowhere to be seen. My sister and I exchanged confused looks, but Mummy was as calm as ever, a true embodiment of grace under pressure. She smiled and took us to our lodgings, where we could freshen up after our long journey. We washed up quickly and headed to the place where lunch would be served.

We were to stay in a thatched basha, something quite magical, exotic, and story-book-like to little me. It was made of mud and straw and was to be our home for the next two to three weeks. It was very different from the comforts of home, but we were eager for whatever lay ahead. We had all our meals at the Officers' Mess, which was also housed in a similar but bigger basha. I felt as though we were living in a fairy tale; I thought myself fortunate and couldn't wait to tell my friends at Delhi all about it upon our return. I couldn't wait to explore and experience the sheer novelty of the local culture and customs. In hindsight, as a grown-up, I feel it is not unlike the travel shows of today where the host stays in exotic locales.

At the Officers' Mess, where we were greeted by a few other aunties and children who were visiting their fathers as well. Being the mischievous duo that we were, we quickly took charge of all the kids, ready for a fun-filled vacation.

Soon, papa arrived and we exulted in his warm embrace as he welcomed us. Such moments were always memorable. The two of us snuggled into his arms and savoured the security we felt in his embrace. I can't help but think how lucky we were to have such a wonderful father who always made us feel loved and special. At that moment, it felt like nothing in the world could bring us down. Our joy knew no bounds.

Mummy and papa's reunion seemed to us like the meeting of sundered hearts; you know, as depicted in movies…only, here, instead of running towards each other and embracing, my father saluted as per military ethos.

Food was always top-notch at the Officers' Mess, and it was no different on this trip. The Gurkha troops, who were famous for their delicious non-vegetarian cuisine, had outdone themselves as usual. Our curiosity led us to explore our surroundings and on one such adventure, we found ourselves behind the Mess kitchen. And that's when we stumbled upon a startling, and somewhat frightening, sight.

A headless chicken came running toward us, and we were both stunned. I presume it was just a reflex action, but at the time we were horrified! We reminisced about this hilarious story for years to come.

Visits to my dad, while he was stationed at field postings, were always adventurous filled with excitement, treats, and lots of fun. After all, who doesn't love spending time with their dad and getting pampered?

The next few days were filled with even more adventure and excitement as we explored the surrounding areas, met papa's local friends, and travelled across the mighty Betar *Nallah*. This rivulet had no bridges and one had to wade across in motorable transport. It was like stepping into a different world. Wading through the *nallah* was the highlight of our trip, as we got to touch the crisp, clear water, and feel the rush of the current as we crossed it in our good old jeep. However, there were times when our little vehicle got stuck in the water and we needed the help of a bigger recovery vehicle, colloquially known as a 3-tonner, to pull us out. It was all part of the thrill of adventure!

Such experiences while growing up made us mindful of the importance of embracing new cultures, making new friends, and taking risks. They have functioned as lessons that have stayed with us for life and shaped us into the curious and fearless individuals we are today. Growing up with a father in the military meant we were always surrounded by excitement and drama.

The thrill of visiting papa and exploring unfamiliar places was something I looked forward to over several summers. A regular highlight of our visits was attending the lively football matches between different sister battalions. The enthusiasm of the officers cheering their teams was contagious, reminding me of the electrifying atmosphere during an India-Pakistan match. And the best part? There was always a dummy airplane next to the football field, just waiting to be explored by curious kids like my sibling and me.

But, as with any childhood, it was not all fun and games. There were lessons to be learned, like respecting the boundaries set by my mother; *like not touching the beehive outside her window!* Even today, I can feel the painful sting of the angry bees that swarmed my face after I ignored her instructions. We were like characters in a Tom and Jerry cartoon, a mischievous duo causing chaos. And then there were the consequences of our mischievous actions, like trying to sneakily steal some *Gulab Jamuns* (Classic Indian sweet) from the waiter serving a VIP guest, only to get caught by papa's sharp eyes, and the rest is history. I won't elaborate more on what happened at that moment; dear reader, use your imagination!

Growing up as a soldier's daughter had its charm; it taught us the values of discipline and patriotism at an incredibly young age. We took part in all regimental events with a lot of enthusiasm, learned the language of our troops, and sang songs that echoed with pride in our hearts. I remember them still…

As our holidays at Poonch ended, we had to leave for Delhi to join school and start a new routine.

Though far too young to understand the gravity of long separations, we were certainly proud of our father who served the nation with honour, and our mother who sacrificed without disparage. Our mother, being the epitome of strength and composure, bid goodbye to our father with a smile, counting the days until she would be reunited with him again. But there were some costs to pay and setbacks, too.

Our father was a tall Sikh Turbaned Gurkha officer over six feet in height. A spirited regimental officer, he was exceedingly proud of his battalion. Apart from being a fit and athletic man, he played volleyball for his battalion. Unfortunately, during one of these matches, he suffered a back injury that left him with a slipped disc.

Despite this setback, my mother remained grateful for our safety, and we moved forward towards new beginnings between our hospital visits. papa was admitted to the hospital for many days, first in Udhampur and later in Base Hospital, Delhi. Despite the slow and challenging recovery, he would make our visits special by giving us treats. However, with time and proper care, he recovered and was soon back on his feet, ready to serve the nation again.

Dilli Calling—1978-1981

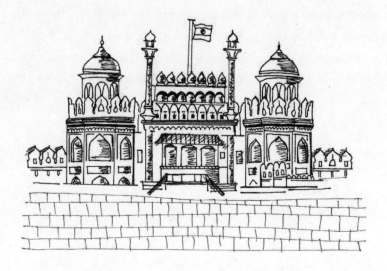

We were overjoyed to hear that our father's regiment was moving lock, stock, and barrel from the northern parts of the country to the capital of India, New Delhi, to be stationed as the President's Bodyguards, a matter of great pride and honour for all of us. *Yaayy!* It seemed to me like a scenario from a presidential thriller with our dad as the ultimate protector. We were now part of a prestigious tradition that dates to the royal era and continues to serve as a symbol of India's rich cultural heritage with a significant place of great pride enjoyed by the Armed Forces.

More significantly, as a family, it also meant staying with our beloved father for two whole years and being able to be with him every single day and night. It was like winning a lottery. Our joy was beyond measure. My grandparents were also relieved, as they wouldn't have to worry about our well-being from afar. Our residence was located inside the grand symbol of Indian history, the magnificent Red Fort. As a UNESCO World Heritage Site, also known as Lal Quila. The fort derives its name from its rich sandstone walls, which have witnessed to travails and high points of the chequered Indian History and stood the test of time.

Our new home was a sprawling vintage bungalow, arranged in four blocks. However, most of the rooms were kept locked or were used for storage. This posed a problem for my petite mother, who was only 5 feet tall, and the door bolts towered over her at 6 feet. To solve this issue, she ingeniously improvised a badminton racket to open and close the doors.

It's funny how memories of this minor inconvenience bring to mind the cultural comparisons from around the world. in some Asian cultures, having small doorways is lucky, as it symbolises protection from evil spirits. In Western cultures, larger doorways are a symbol of wealth and prosperity.

This reminds of a popular meme where a person is too short to reach the top shelf, and their friend must assist them. If only my tall papa was around to assist her! It brings a light-heartedness to the story, and I can't help but smile when I think about it.

One night, we were in for quite a surprise. A deadly cobra made an unexpected visit to our parents' washroom. Very Indiana Jones! The magnificent creature was coiled in the sink, staring straight at my father. But papa, the very embodiment of courage, managed to safely escort the cobra out of our home, with the help of a trusted friend. My mother was paranoid about creepy crawlies...so what on earth would she have done had she been greeted by King Cobra, way deadlier than a mere creepy-crawly? Thankfully, she was kept in the dark about the incident, as the sight of a cobra in the washroom would have sent her running a sprint marathon in the middle of the night.

Our new home was also home to a lively community of Gurkha troops. These troops were very fond of their company commander—my father, who spoke their dialect and shared their love for food, especially the non-vegetarian cuisine. The area was teeming with pigeons, some of which would often end up as lunch in the rooms of the troops. The smell of freshly prepared delicacies would fill the air, and my father would always comment on the fact that the troops had put their *gulel* (a traditional wooden toy comprising a Y-shaped stick with elastic between the arms, used for propelling small stones—a catapult) to effective use. The scene was almost reminiscent of the famous 'Where's the beef?' meme, with my father playfully teasing the troops about their hunting skills.

Sibling rivalry is a universal phenomenon that knows no bounds and affects households across cultures and continents. My sister and I were no exception to this. We constantly bickered and battled over the smallest of things. We would be engaging in fistfights and kickboxing, this drove our parents to the brink of insanity. I vividly recall the day when our constant arguments finally touched the boiling point and our father decided that he had had enough. We were issued an ultimatum to pack our bags and leave the house if we did not improve our behaviour. Thinking that our parents were seriously angry with us, both solemnly—discussed viable alternate arrangements and options. We were considering moving to our grandmother's house when, to our surprise, we found our parents standing right behind us, silently watching and laughing at our seriously mature discussions.

As the adage goes, 'children should be seen and not heard;' in our case, it was more like 'children are always heard and rarely seen.' The competitive spirit between siblings is a normal part of growing up and can even be comically portrayed in meme culture. But at the end of the day, it's all good fun and is just a small chapter in the grand story of siblinghood.

As the children of the regiment, we were some of the lucky few to have been offered to attend the prestigious Delhi Public School, Mathura Road. My first introduction to the world of uniforms was in Grade-1. I remember feeling proud and grown up as I put on my crisp white shirt, green skirt, and shiny black shoes. I suppose I must have looked pretty smug, for my younger sister, who was admitted to the junior wing of the school, was disappointed to find out that there was no uniform requirement. How was it possible for her to be left behind? It took a little more than persistent cajoling from my parents to convince the school authorities to make an exception and allow my sibling to wear the uniform, making her the only one in the nursery wing to do so.

Every morning, the Delhi Transport Corporation school bus would pick us up from the Red Fort main gate amidst the chilly winter air of Delhi. Guardsmen, chauffeurs, and other service providers would often be seen huddled around small fires, warming their hands and wrapping themselves in shawls and blankets, trying to protect themselves from the proverbially famous '*Dilli Ki Sardi*' (the cold of Delhi). Our bus ride to school was always a fascinating journey, taking us through the bustling streets of Delhi, passing by the *Jama-Masjid* mosque, where the morning prayers could be heard in the background.

As we travelled to school, I couldn't help but compare my experiences to those of my friends in different parts of the world. From the freezing cold winters in Delhi to the scorching hot summers in Australia, each place has its own unique culture and weather. And who says learning must be boring? I recall the way kids used to laugh at Gini for sporting a uniform, but I was secretly happy that she had ensured she got what she wanted.

My childhood memories of attending Delhi Public School, Mathura Road will forever be ingrained in my mind. From the proud feeling of wearing my first uniform to the fascinating bus rides through the heart of Delhi, these memories will always bring a smile to my face. Fridays were always a highlight of my week, as it meant leaving behind the  homework and tests of the school week and embarking on a thrilling ride with my family to my grandma's (*Nani's)* house. I would stand in front of my papa's old but very reliable *'Humara Bajaj'* scooter, with the wind blowing through my hair, while my mother sat behind and my young sister, Gini, sat crossed-legged on her lap. Mummy would be consistently trying to keep both Gini and me from falling asleep, as I was precariously at the front and Gini was sandwiched between both parents. Admittedly, it sounds scary, but hey, Mummy was a rock star! We were always safe under her vigilant eye.

Nani's house was a hub of family reunions. Bustling with activity, it was a place full of love with cousins, aunts, uncles, and grandparents, all gathering for regular family rituals that *Nani* encouraged. The idea behind these gatherings was to foster strong bonds within the family, something that *Nani* believed was essential for a close-knit family. Sunday mornings were spent glued to the television, watching the evergreen Star Trek series, with its tales of human adventures 'where no man had ever gone before'. There used to be a joke that the place was the ladies' loo! Back then, the television was like a magic box, with shutters that could be locked to prevent anyone from sneaking a peek.

After the thrilling tele-series, the aroma of delicious and simple food would waft through the house, signalling it was time for lunch. Warm ghee being readied for the final tadka (tempering), unfailingly, made me aware of a hole in my tummy waiting to be filled with *Nani ka Khana*. The whole family would gather around my grandfather's eight-seater dining table, savouring every bite of her delicious home-cooked meal. One of my favourite memories was of *Nani's* mango ice cream, made in her customised aluminium ice trays, with huge satisfying chunks of mango to bite into.

Nani's house only had two bedrooms; so, whenever the whole family got together, there would be a spillover of people sleeping in the living room on spare cotton mattresses laid out on the floor. The nights were filled with nonstop chatting and giggling; and on some occasions, the children would refuse to sleep early. To scare us into bed, my aunts, my mother's younger sisters, would tell us about the bogeyman '*Chunni*

Lal'. This was followed by a pin-drop silence. A chance whistle from the streets or sometimes a loud bang of bamboo on the road would make us shriek and yell and then the lights would go off, finally sending us to slumberland.

Growing up with my cousins, we always tried to have a bit of harmless fun and adventure. One such memorable episode was during a sleepover at *Nani's* house. My cousins and I took turns jumping in and out of bed. When it was my cousin Sovina's turn, I jokingly suggested she try jumping backward. Little did I know that this silly suggestion would lead to a trip to the doctor. As Sovina attempted jumping, she lost her balance and her face hit the edge of the bed, resulting in a gash on her forehead that needed stitches.

Another time, on a typical summer day in Delhi, my sister Gini and I were lounging around our grandparents' house, trying to come up with ingenious ways to pass our time. We were both stir-crazy and looking for excitement. That's when

I decided to climb the dressing table in Nani's bedroom. The table was like a military-style dresser, with a large mirror that took up most of the surface. I know now that it was a ridiculous idea, but back then to a kid at a naughty age

like me, thoroughly bored and infused with a burning desire to push boundaries and explore, it was a fun thing to attempt.

As we were climbing, we were cautious; but gradually confidence took over, and that was when disaster struck—the mirror suddenly came crashing down, with a deafening noise, freezing us both in place and creating a loud noise that echoed throughout the house. Although we were both unharmed, the mirror was shattered into a million pieces, much to the shock of everyone who came running to the room. Gini started to cry, and I could feel my eyes welling up too. We had done something seriously wrong, and we knew it.

Looking back now, I can't help but laugh at how silly we were, but at the time it was a scary but learning experience, part of growing up. It taught me a valuable lesson about looking before I leapt.

Such moments always bring back fond memories of our childhood, full of laughter and mischief. It's a reminder of the innocence and pure joy that kids emanate. I often reflect on these moments and can't help but smile at the silly experiences we shared. Silly, yes; but what fun!

As a young child growing up in Delhi, my most unforgettable memories of the delectable *ghar ka khana* that my grandmother, *(Nani)*, would prepare at home, to the impromptu plans of feasting on Biriyani at India Gate, followed by huge dollops of Gaylord ice cream at Connaught Place for everyone. These sensorial remembrances are ingrained in my very being, still making me delight in warm aromas and rich flavours as I recall them.

How can anyone forget the incredible pineapple ice cream that my father used to make with his wooden ice cream machine? Every time we had cousins visiting us, he'd whip up batch after batch of the sweet, tropical treat. It was a remarkable sight and a flavour to crave, as he expertly churned away, creating a dessert that was simply out of this world. He never failed to amaze everyone with his skills, churning out scoop upon scoop until his guests would have to raise their hands in surrender, pleading with him to *please stop!* Of course, we eagerly awaited such gatherings and occasions!

I remember being diagnosed with chicken pox and having to be isolated from my younger sister. No matter how hard our parents tried to keep us apart, we both faced the wrath of chicken pox together and despite being sick, the excitement of exploring new things never faded. During our recovery, my sister and I stumbled upon a secret entry point to the light and sound show inside the gardens of the Red Fort in Delhi. Every evening, we would sit in awe as the massive ramparts of the historic fort came to life with the sound and light show.

Watching the light and sound show at the Red Fort was a surreal experience, reminding me of the grandeur and magnificence of the Mughal Empire. It's amazing how a simple visit to a historical site can transport you back in time, making you feel like a part of a different era.

My papa was a gem of a person. He had an incredible memory and was a walking encyclopaedia of all the historical events and data related to his battalion. He was a proud soldier, always taking pride in his regiment and his troops. He was so enthusiastic about preserving the history of his battalion that he voluntarily took pride in writing memoirs, anecdotes, service digest, annotating and maintaining the official history of his regiment—a task entrusted only to a few officers with a gift for writing. He took pride in learning about the silverware—papa had a penchant for finding out about the history of every silver trophy and piece of cutlery possessed by the battalion. Any recent addition would further raise curiosity in him. Consequently, or it could be because of this particular interest, it fell into his lap to set up the Officers' Mess whenever the *paltan* (Battalion) moved. He knew the regimental customs and his men well.

Papa's love for writing would not stop there. He would go on to author five books and establish his own publishing house 25 years later. He was not only knowledgeable but also had a profound sense of humour. Papa was known for his hilarious remarks, rib-tickling jokes, and making everyone around him laugh. He was a true storyteller, always keeping his audience engaged and entertained. It is from here that I would later take inspiration to pursue my interests and passions.

One memorable afternoon, my father shared the exciting news that his battalion would support the road traffic management and assistance to the Republic Day Parade. We would be privy to the final dress rehearsal of the grand parade and just like the previous year, we had the honour of observing the Independence Day ceremony from the ramparts of the Red Fort followed by a dinner hosted by none other than the President (*Rashtrapati*) who is also the Supreme Commander of the Indian Armed Forces.

As my parents arrived at the official reception hosted at *Rashtrapati Bhavan (Official residence of the President of India)*, the first address in the country, I remember mummy being overwhelmed by the grandiosity of the place, a feeling which she often recalled and reminisced on later. The then Hon'ble President of India, Neelam Sanjeeva Reddy was in attendance, and it was decided that a group photograph with the officers would be taken. Unfortunately, my father was attending to something and missed the opportune moment. Boy! He didn't let that stop him. He shouted out loudest from behind, "Wait! I wasn't in the previous one. Could we do it all over again?" There was a moment of silence before President Sanjeeva Reddy turned around, looked at my father, and with a smile said, "Let's do it for the young officer!" This incident reminds me of a similar incident in the movie 'The Devil Wears Prada,' where Miranda Priestly, the Editor-In-Chief, stops the entire shoot just to have her assistant included in a group photo.

This moment also reminded me of a popular meme where a person says 'I wasn't ready' before a group photo is taken. But in this case, my father was ready and made sure he didn't miss the opportunity for a photo with the President. This experience was not just about a group photo, but about the humility and graciousness of our Honourable President. This is what I learned from my parents to be honest and to speak my mind, even if it meant speaking up in a formal and potentially intimidating setting like a Presidential Reception.

But despite his playful nature, papa was also a person of firm principles. If he didn't approve of someone, he would tell them straight to their face. For him, there were no grey areas, only black and white. He lived his life with integrity and always kept his heart free of negative emotions. A man of his stature and character is truly rare to come by.

Dill-Jan-Assam 1981

O ur time in Delhi seemed to have flashed by and before we knew, it was time for another goodbye, for us to bid adieu to the Red Fort, our cousins, and to everything that made up our Delhi experience. We learned that our next destination was a place called Dinjan (which my father deliberately pronounced as *Diljaan* (Heart and Soul), perhaps in a positively emotive way). It was a place we had never heard of, so we eagerly opened a map to find out where it was located. The journey involved a long train trip of three nights and four days, with a train change at New Bongaigaon because of the rail tracks converting from broad gauge to meter gauge. Indeed, it was a vastly different era from the rail journeys of today defined by Rajdhani, Vande Bharat, and the soon-to-arrive Bullet Train—boy, we sure have come a long way! We were thrilled about the prospect of a long train journey, but our parents had their concerns, including the monumental task of packing and moving our belongings.

On the day of departure, our family and friends gathered at the Old Delhi railway station to say goodbye. In those days, relatives and friends were more in number than the ones travelling. Unfortunately, our plans were interrupted when the train was cancelled because of the Assam Bandh. There was unrest at the destination state of Assam. The new departure time remained uncertain as we returned from the railway station not once, but several times in the coming days. Finally, my father decided it would be best to say our goodbyes at home rather than have our well-wishers come to the station every day and repeat the emotional family drama in a public place just like a soap opera for everyone to see and relish. After several false alarms, we finally set off on our journey a week later than planned.

The trip to the destination took us across various states, unveiling the mysteries that the child in me would never forget. We crossed the massive Brahmaputra River, which resembled an unending ocean. The journey was filled with adventures and experiences that are forever etched in my memory. This journey was not just about moving from one place to another, but about the thrill of discovering unfamiliar places and learning on the go.

Let me now attempt to take you on that delightful journey to the mesmerising northeastern parts of India, where our path wound through endless tea gardens, lush green rice fields, and banana trees adorned with the sweetest, pocket-sized bananas you've ever seen! Our destination was Tinsukia, the major town nearest to our place of residence.

As I stepped off the train at the Tinsukia railway station, I was filled with a mixture of excitement and nerves. This small station in the heart of a region filled with gardens and forests of different hues would be a half-hour drive from my home for the next two years, and I was eager to start this new chapter of my life. However, my excitement was short-lived as I soon realised that our luggage, including my mother's precious shawls and silk saris, had been stolen at the New Bongaigaon station. Our grandparents rushed across new dresses and winterwear for us. Despite this setback, my mother remained grateful for our safety, and we moved forward toward new beginnings.

As we approached our cantonment, the anticipation built, and I cannot help but smile at the vivid imagery that still comes to mind as I reminisce. The military station was nestled in the heart of a picturesque landscape, surrounded by vast tea gardens that stretched as far as the eye could see. Those tea gardens weren't just any ordinary gardens; for us kids, they were like fairy tale lands filled with colourful flowers and mesmerising secrets waiting to be discovered.

The tea gardens are the crown jewel of this enchanting region. As we drove through the undulating hills covered in emerald, green tea bushes, the air was infused with the sweet scent of tea leaves. It was as if nature itself had brewed a fragrant cup of tea for us to savour at every turn! And oh, the tea pluckers! We spotted them skilfully picking the tea leaves, moving gracefully between the bushes like dancers in a choreographed performance. Their nimble fingers moved with lightning speed, and it was both fascinating and amusing to watch them work their magic. We waved and smiled at them, trying to match their speed with our clumsy attempts to mimic their actions.

As we reached Dinjan, the military cantonment held a vast campus. It was a bustling little community with all the facilities one could dream of those days. Indeed, it was a mini adventure town in the heart of the tea gardens. The camaraderie among the families living there created a warm and welcoming atmosphere. Children from various backgrounds came together, forming friendships as diverse and vibrant as the campus surrounding them.

Amidst the beauty of this region, we found joy in the simple pleasures of life. From picnics in the gardens, where we sprawled under the shade of tea bushes, pretending they were our secret treks, to climbing trees and huddling up to share adventure stories—every day felt like an exciting chapter in a whimsical storybook.

The most noteworthy aspect of this period was that all children in the small military station went to the same school. This was in stark contrast to my previous experiences, where everyone was used to being in different schools. Despite this, I was eager to make new friends and learn more about the place I would call home for the next couple of years.

The makeshift school we attended was housed in a few old barracks that had been converted for educational purposes. Assam experiences heavy rainfall and flooding. As a result, our classroom was often flooded in knee-deep waters. When this happened, our school would promptly declare a rainy-day holiday. But, despite these challenges, I quickly grew to love school and the teachers, who were all local aunties. For them, tutoring the young children was a way to fulfil their career aspirations and opportunities, as there were limited career choices in the remote and rural area in which we were based.

The time spent at Tinsukia was a unique and memorable experience that taught me the importance of adapting to new environments and forming strong relationships with the surrounding people. I was grateful for the opportunity this special place provided me with learning and growing in so many ways.

Every Friday was a day to look forward to. Invariably, we would head to the garrison cinema hall in the campus to catch the latest movie—in those good old days, movies were the highlights of our lives! Our movie hall was just a stone's throw away from home. Fridays were especially exciting, as it was the "free show" day. This was our Friday night ritual at the nearby movie hall—free movies and a frenzy for seats. That meant securing our seats was like a mission impossible, but we were determined, armed with whatever we could find in our hands—umbrellas, hankies, and I even remember one time when my friend tried to block our seats with her homework notebook!

Imagine hilarious chaos: kids racing around like whirlwinds, staking claims with their tiny treasures. Umbrellas tangled, hankies airborne, my friend shielding her notebook like a prized possession from a toddler's grasp. Chaos ruled, adults stared, but oh, the sweet taste of victory! Looking back, it's a memory brimming with humour and camaraderie, but guess what? We were an army of mischievous, determined youngsters, unfazed by grown-up glares; in fact, they fuelled our rebellious spirits. Once victorious in the seat battle, high-fives were exchanged with secret-agent intensity, and giggles spread like wildfire. The cinema turned into a kid-packed arena, anticipation electrifying the air. The movie hall was our battleground, united in pursuit of cinematic thrills. Despite the chaos and stern glances, we revelled in a sense of achievement, young warriors on an entertainment quest. Then, the lights flickered on—a collective hush, charged with excitement, punctuated by bursts of giddy cheers.

Of course, in those days, there was no fancy surround sound or reclining seats like today. But that didn't matter to us. We were living our best lives, and the movies were our escape from reality. We would laugh, cry, and cheer along with the characters on the screen, completely lost in the magic of cinema.

Looking back, it's funny to think how we used to fight for those seats and the chaos we created in the name of securing them. But it was all part of the fun and the thrill of those Friday free shows. They were the highlight of our week, and those memories still bring a smile to my face.

At other times, we would make a trip to the nearby town of Digboi, the birthplace of the first oil well in Asia. This place held a special place in our hearts, not just because of its rich history, but also because of the scenic beauty that surrounded it.

Continuing with the thrilling series of deputations and tours my father had to travel to - we had the opportunity to visit some of the most breathtaking places in the region, such as the valley of Arunachal Pradesh, the land of cloud-kissed peaks, (known as the England of the East) and the lush green jungles of Lekhapani, Zero, Shillong, Teju, Jairampur,

Lekhabali, Along and Walong. Each remote place we visited was unique - cocooned in the remotest corners of the Indian eastern state of Arunachal Pradesh.

Every state had its unique topography. Assam had the mighty river, the banana plantations, and the lush green tea gardens, whereas Arunachal Pradesh had steep and treacherous climbs, deep jungles, and, little villages and beautiful peaks veiled in low clouds. Northeastern states have a beautiful sunrise, and the day breaks as early as 4 a.m., and the night falls in early, dusk and sunset around 5 p.m. I just can't forget the creepy crawlies that were in abundance—Gini had a leech in her socks one day and our domestic help had one on her neck.

One of the most memorable experiences of my childhood was crossing the mighty Brahmaputra River on a ferry that could carry enormous trucks and heavy equipment. As the sun set on the horizon, we would watch in awe as the dolphins danced on the tranquil waters, and the vast expanse of the river seemed to stretch on forever. These experiences were nothing short of magical, and I felt truly blessed to have had the chance to witness the beauty of our world first-hand.

During this time, I recall my mother's battle with severe asthma. It was a challenging time for our family, especially for her, as she struggled to breathe properly. To get her the best possible treatment, she was flown to Delhi via Kolkata (Calcutta) for further medical attention. For us kids, however, it was even more fun and exciting as we were to travel by air, from Dinjan to Calcutta (a first for us in those days when it was not only rare but also prohibitively expensive.) We were indeed anxious and happy, especially since, thereafter, we would take the Rajdhani Express (A train that had seats, was interconnected, and air-conditioned) upto Delhi, which seemed like an extension of our air travel.

My father, who always had a way of making us feel comfortable, explained to us that in case we felt any discomfort during the flight, we needed to blow the air out of our ears. Although I still don't understand what that meant, it definitely made us feel a little better. The popular music number "*Disco Diwane*" by Pakistani singer Nazia Hassan was playing on the loop inside the train, making the journey even more enjoyable. She was a Pakistani singer and songwriter, who was popularly known as the Queen of South Asian pop among the young Indians in the1980s.

When we arrived in Delhi, my mother was diagnosed with chronic asthma and was advised to stay in Delhi, which had a dryer climate, till the time she felt better. However, we had to go back to Tinsukia as the summer break was soon to end and schools were about to start. Our father did his best to make sure we didn't miss our mother too much. He took on the dual role of father and mother, cooking for us and braiding our hair in topknots and securing them neatly with U-pins. It eventually became a fashion statement in our school. Papa was looked upon as the coolest dad around. He made us prepare for our exams, took us to movies, for swimming, and made sure we were looked after.

The Dinjan station became like an extended family for us, with everyone pampering us and making sure we were happy living up to the nickname Diljaan coined by papa! Even after all these years, many of the friends we made during this time have reconnected, reminding us of the special bond we all shared during that time.

One afternoon, my papa received an exciting assignment—to travel to the enchanting hill station of Shillong in the state of Meghalaya. Dubbed the "Fashion Capital of the East," Shillong was a four-hour journey away from Guwahati, which itself was about five hours from Dinjan. Gini and I, including our house help, were packed up in a one-ton army vehicle, ready for an adventure, complete with bedding in the back for us to catch some shut-eye during the journey.

As we arrived in Shillong, the weather was perfect, with blooming flowers and bustling markets, and we soon settled into our holiday home. The next day, as papa had official work to attend to, papa's friend Col. Shenoy arrived on his scooter and took us, along with his own children, on a scenic tour of the city, starting with a visit to the famous Shillong Peak and the local zoo. A scene to remember with four little children sitting on a two-wheeler. Col Shenoy became our local guide. *What fun!*

When we returned home to Dinjan, we were overjoyed to hear that our mummy was finally coming back to us. Mummy came back and normalcy returned to our home.

Mummy had a green thumb, and our home was always adorned with exotic plants and flowers. We even grew some of the sweetest strawberries and pineapples in our backyard, which we would send to our relatives. She was a qualified interior decorator and a fine arts graduate. Mummy had a special talent for flower arrangements. However, due to her chronic asthma, she had been advised to stay away from fresh flowers and instead, she focused on arranging dry flowers, a talent that she passed down to my sister and me. I can almost feel Mummy's smile from beyond whenever my sister or I create a beautiful flower arrangement in our own homes. It is an imperishable tradition that connects us to her, and the memories of our childhood.

Dehradun Beckons—1984

Ic was the early 1980s, and the world was transforming. The military was a tight-knit community, and as an army kid, I became used to travelling with parents, moving around every few years. This time, our destination was Dehradun in Uttarakhand. The city was nestled between two of the largest rivers in India, The Ganges and The Yamuna, and was known for its stunning scenery and rich culture.

As we prepared to leave Dinjan after a small break in Delhi, papa was temporarily stationed in Roorkee, a small town *en route* to Dehradun, while the rest of his regiment was preparing to join him in Dehradun. My mother, my sister, and I arrived a few days later and were welcomed by family friends, who graciously offered to let us stay with her.

Back then, hotels and *Airbnb* were not yet a thing, and finding a place to stay was a challenge. The idea of staying in a hotel was not even considered, and the unspoken understanding between friends was to help each other out during these transitional periods. We were lucky to have my mother's friend and her family to rely on, and it was a reminder of the strong bonds that exist in the military community.

Fast forward 40 years, I was reunited with my childhood aunt, my kind friend, in Delhi, and it was a surreal experience. As often happens in *fauj*, her son-in-law and my future husband were colleagues in the same office and good friends. Her daughter Anupama has kept in touch with us even after moving to Canberra, Australia. This is a testament to the unbreakable ties that we formed as army kids.

Looking back on this time, I realise how lucky I was to have grown up in a family that valued relationships and community. In a world where everything seems so transitory, transactional, and temporary, the memories and bonds formed during our army adventures have stood the test of time.

As I recall, life in Dehradun was full of delight and new experiences. One day, a young officer who was leaving for a short course offered us a unique opportunity to make ourselves comfortable despite not having been allotted a house. He wound up his entire household into one room and gave us the use of his house until we found a place of our own. This selfless act of kindness was not an uncommon occurrence in those days when the military community was tight-knit and looked after each other like family.

As we settled into our new surroundings, my sister and I started school, eager to make new friends and explore this beautiful city in the foothills of the Himalayas, surrounded by the mighty rivers of the Ganges and Yamuna.

One day, as we were out and about in the town, we noticed a three-wheeler following us and its passengers waving wildly at us. At first, we thought it was just someone having fun, so we waved back. Little did we know it was our papa who had returned from an assignment and wanted to surprise us. In typical army child fashion, we played along and led him on a

tour of half the town before he
popped out to
reveal that it was
him and realised
why the vehicle
was following
us with a
frantically
waving
occupant. That
surprise
reunion was
memorable
and brings a smile to my face to
this day.

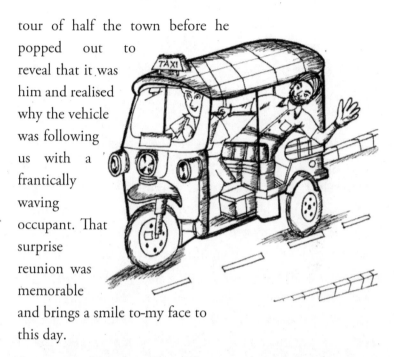

A young girl by then, I vividly remember passing by a very impressive but enigmatic-looking school campus on our way to the town. The towering gates were intimidating in an effective way and emanated an aura of mystery. We were told that the boys who attended this school were admitted to the hostel at an early age of 11-12 years in the 7th grade and were prepared to join the Armed Forces. This was something that made my mother feel a sense of sympathy towards these young children, whom she imagined must be missing their parents dearly. But little did we know at that time that this school would end up being an integral part of most of my adult life.

Fifteen years later, I found myself marrying one of the boys from that school and joining the esteemed Rimcollian community. For the uninitiated, RIMC alumni or Rimcollians are those who graduate from the school (RIMC) formerly known as Prince of Wales... Royal Indian Military College. It is a feeder institution for the National Defence Academy.

It was a warm evening in 1984, and my parents were shopping near the clock tower on their scooter when suddenly the town downed its shutters. Word went around that a tragic incident had taken place involving Mrs Indira Gandhi, the then-Hon'ble Prime Minister. Following her tragic assassination, the northern part of our country witnessed one of the most violent riots. The next few months were a tumultuous time, filled with uncertainty and confusion. My father had to leave for Delhi for the anti-riot duty while we stayed behind. He was in the capital city for an extended period, and those were some of the most challenging times we have faced as a family.

Upon returning, my father one day announced that he had made the bold decision to go back to college and pursue his graduation. He was an alumnus of the National Defence Academy, but not a graduate, as in those days the academy had no affiliation or tie up with the Jawaharlal Nehru University for a parallel graduation degree. He enrolled as a student in the local college and embarked on a journey of self-discovery and education. This meant attending tutorials in the evenings while balancing his professional responsibilities, which were virtually a 24-hour commitment. To some who remember, my father could think and write at a supersonic speed simultaneously.

The students in his class were half his age, and they affectionately referred to him as *'Uncleji'*. (Suffix used to give respect). Soon my father became the favourite *Uncleji* of the class and despite the age difference, quickly assumed cult status as a guide, mentor, and a popular friend. He was always eager to help his young friends, assisting them with their English notes and even helping draft love letters for aspiring Romeos in the class. His kind and approachable nature made him an invaluable resource for his peers. As he progressed through his studies, my father quickly proved that age was just a number and that one could always learn and grow, regardless of how old one was. This was especially evident when he graduated in First Class, proving that dedication and hard work always pays off.

Not only did papa achieve his personal goal, but the favourite *"Uncle ji"* also played a significant role in bringing together the aspiring young lovers in his class. His presence had a positive impact on the students, showing them that wisdom and experience can come from unexpected places.

In a world where ageism can be rampant, my father's story is a testament to the fact that it's never too late to learn and grow. I draw inspiration from his journey and find solace that there are people out there who can help bridge the gap between generations. And of course, I cannot forget to mention the occasional humour that my father would use to lighten the mood in the classroom, showing that the ability to laugh and see the funny side of things goes a long way in relieving moments of tension or awkwardness.

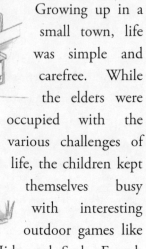

Growing up in a small town, life was simple and carefree. While the elders were occupied with the various challenges of life, the children kept themselves busy with interesting outdoor games like Hide and Seek, French Cricket, *Gulli-Danda*, *Pitthu*, and cycling.

We were completely oblivious to the world beyond our little campus, but we lived in the moment, cherishing each day and the simple pleasures that came with it.

One of the most exciting life-changing events that happened during this time was the introduction of Colour Television. Our neighbour, Bose Auntie, had the luxury of owning one. Children in our neighbourhood would sneak into her house just to see the amazing technicolour display. It was a time of simple pleasures. Watching addictive soap operas like "*Buniyaad*" and "*Hum Log*" was the ultimate in-home entertainment. Sundays were reserved for the epic mythological serial "Ramayana." It was indeed the beginning of the era of small-screen entertainment that had just set its foot in India. Technology was slowly invading our lives, changing the way we lived and interacted with the world.

Our mothers were the ultimate support system of our childhood, always taking care of us and ensuring we had everything we needed. They spent their days at home in mundane activities, knitting sweaters, making delicious food, and chatting with friends – all this while ensuring that they maintained complete situational awareness of all our doings and undoing. In addition, they also took care of the soldiers' families. Everyone could speak and understand the language of their troops. Our group of friends was in the age range of ten to fifteen years, and we were carefree and innocent, completely unaware of the complexities of adult life.

One special memory that stands out from my childhood was my tenth birthday. I was a popular kid on my campus, Birpur Cantt and everyone who knew me wished me. I, on my part, had invited all of them to the house for a birthday party. The day was filled with joy and laughter, and the birthday party was a grand affair, with people coming from everywhere to celebrate with me. However, I knew little of the effort that went into organising the party. My mother, who managed everything, had worked tirelessly to make sure everything was perfect without the support of Amazon, Swiggy etc, which were unheard of then. Looking back now, I realise how difficult it must have been for her, but she did it all with love and a smile on her face.

Growing up in a small town had some drawbacks too. For instance, family members and relatives were far away. We had to travel a considerable distance to get essentials, and public transport was not always accessible; but it was a beautiful experience, filled with fond memories. We became a close-knit family within the Cantt. Our schools were nearby, and everybody knew everybody. Help was always nearby. In a world where technology has now taken over our lives, it is nice to look back and recall a simpler time, when the most important things in life were the people, we loved and the memories we created together.

As I entered my adolescent years, I found myself surrounded by friends who were experiencing the physical changes that come with puberty. It seemed like every day someone had a new story to share about their period, and I couldn't help feeling a little left out. It felt like having your period was the key to being considered an "adult" among our group of friends, and I was eager to join in.

One day, I mustered up the courage to talk to my mother about it. I told her I was feeling like the odd one out and that I wanted to start my period so that I could be a part of the "cool club". My mother just chuckled and told me that my body would change when it was ready. I was not convinced.

The next morning, it happened and I actually experienced it before leaving for school. My mother was packing our lunches, and I confided in her about my worries. She listened sympathetically and reassured me that everything would settle down in its own time.

Later that day, my father picked me up from school, and I could tell that my mother had talked to him about my concerns. As soon as I walked in the door, my little sister Gini excitedly told me about the latest game she had learned to play with her friends. My father interrupted her and told her I was growing up and that it was time for her to think about growing up as well. I could see that Gini got the message, and I was relieved that my parents were there to support me through this confusing and often awkward stage in life.

I remember a time when my father went on an exercise to Rajasthan from Delhi. He was away for a month or two, and we only received updates from uncles who visited us from where he was. This was in the days before mobile phones, and letters typically took a long time to get delivered, so we were in the dark about his well-being. One day, a friend of his narrated an incident that happened during a conference. My father felt a slight movement on his stomach and initially thought it was his belt, only to realise he wasn't wearing one that day. When he looked down, he saw a poisonous Krait snake, basking in the warmth of his body. My father, forever the cool-headed one, took out his handkerchief and, in a split second, threw the snake into the centre of the gathering. It was given a safe passage by those present.

However, in total contrast, when my mother listened to the story, she kept repeating "*Waheguru Waheguru*", a sacred Sikh chant thanking the Almighty. It is worth noting that she was phobic about snakes, so this incident must have scared the living daylight out of her.

Danapur, Bihar & Siliguri, West Bengal— 1986-1989

S oon after my father's return from the exercise, he broke to us the exciting news of our transfer to Danapur, a satellite town of Patna in the State of Bihar, as the Zonal Recruiting Officer responsible for drafting young boys as recruit soldiers in the Indian Army. Danapur was known as Dinapur during the British period. The word Dinapur means the "City of Grains," being located in the fertile Gangetic plains. Established in 1765, Danapur Cantonment is the second-oldest cantonment in the country. It was the only white cantonment of the East India Company at one point of time, and the largest military cantonment in Bengal. Located on the southern banks of the Ganga, Danapur was chosen, perhaps due to the availability of an inland water route to Calcutta through the Ganga. The Cantonment also played a crucial role in the freedom struggle of 1857, as on 25 July 1857 sepoys of the garrison revolted against the British.

Not much, however, is documented about the lawlessness, goonda raj and the Thakur culture that prevailed in Bihar those days. Being responsible for providing coveted government jobs to young men, it was to be one of the most challenging peace time assignments for my father. Oblivious of the challenges of professional life and adulthood, me and my sister were excited and looked forward to living in yet another new place, going to a new school and making new friends.

My father set off with our truck from Dehradun carrying the household goods, but unfortunately, the driver fell ill *en-route*, a situation which had the potential of disastrous consequences in those days of lawless Bihar. Never the one to be deterred, he took control of the steering wheel and ended up driving more than half the distance. Another example of his initiative, quick and bold decision-making, and his outstanding leadership traits.

When it was our turn to finally arrive in Danapur, we had to change trains at Mughalsarai junction. As we made our way through the platform with many suitcases, boxes, bags, and our dog Pedro, my mother couldn't help but notice the curious onlookers who were gawking at the sheer number of belongings we had with us. My mother, never one to shy away from a challenge, scolded the onlookers and asked, "Haven't you seen people moving on transfers before?" She then shooed them away, much to the amusement of those nearby.

This situation can be compared to the great migrations of animals, where entire herds or flocks move from one place to another, often with their young and all their belongings in tow. Just like wildebeests or caribou, my family was making our way to a new home, and we were determined to take all our worldly possessions with us.

But, in a more light-hearted vein, it's also reminiscent of the classic "When you're moving in the Army and your entire life is packed in boxes" meme. The scene of my mother shooing away the onlookers, with all our belongings scattered around us, is the epitome of a chaotic move so typical of a *fauji* family peacetime manoeuvre!

Arriving at a new place is always exciting, and setting up our new home was no less than an adventure. My mom, being particular about milk, asked around for suggestions, and a friendly neighbour recommended fresh buffalo milk. We thought, "Why not? Let's try it." The next morning, at the crack of dawn, we were greeted with the sound of a bell ringing at 7 a.m. Still half-asleep, we stumbled to the door, only to find a villager standing there with a bucket in one hand and a buffalo right behind him, munching on some grass. With an announcement *"Madam jee, Bhainswaji aa gayee"*! (Buffalo has arrived)

Yes, you read that right. "Fresh", meant that he would milk the buffalo right there at our doorstep. It was both hilarious and shocking. We weren't used to having buffalo around as a part of our morning routine.

But wait, it gets even funnier. Our Dachshund, Pedro, would have none of it. He was barking like crazy, running in circles around the buffalo, and trying to chase it away. The poor villager was taken aback, not knowing how to deal with this tiny, feisty dog.

We tried to calm Pedro down, but he was having none of it. He saw that buffalo as an intruder, and he was determined to protect us from it. Every morning, the same scene would replay itself — the villager with his bucket, the buffalo waiting patiently, and Pedro going berserk.

Eventually, we had to find a workaround. We asked the villager to milk the buffalo a little farther from our doorstep, where Pedro couldn't see it. That way, we would get our fresh milk, and Pedro could peacefully continue with his morning nap.

In the end, it turned out to be quite an amusing and unforgettable experience. We had never imagined that getting fresh buffalo milk would involve such a comical morning show with Pedro as the star performer. It just goes to show that sometimes surprises in life can bring the most laughter.

Our home and new school had a common boundary wall. The first day at my new school in Danapur was filled with amusement as I was given a moniker by the teachers and students, who referred to me as *"Chad... Haaaaji* Ji," in a sing-song tone and I found it hilarious that my surname had become a part-time pet name. It was a sign of respect and camaraderie, and I quickly made many friends who would eventually become lifelong companions.

One of the perks of my new school was that its proximity allowed me to come home for a hot lunch during the break. Mummy had made it easier still, by placing a ladder for the ease of jumping across to school. It is where I would take turns to join my friends Archana, Jagdish, Sanjay, Vihag, Nipun, Meenakshi, Sanjay

Malik, and many others for a delicious meal. We all had a lot of fun together that would never be forgotten.

Upon jumping I could hear boys shouting in their local dialect *"Whoh Kude Chadhaji,"* which translates to, "Here jumps Chadhaji." It became a slogan that was shouted out every time I jumped over the wall.

One bright sunny morning, a villager came to my father and asked if he could climb a particular tree in our garden. My father, always eager to help, said yes, and within a few  minutes, the man had climbed the tree and attached a terracotta pot to the top. When asked what it was, the man replied, *"Tari."*

This was a traditional fermented juice extract from the bark of the tree that would accumulate inside the pot and eventually turn into an intoxicating drink relished by the locals.

This experience can be compared to the tradition of making wine or cider in many cultures around the world. Just as people in Italy or France might ferment grapes to make wine, this villager was using the tree in our garden to make his own unique drink.

In a lighter vein, the image of the villager climbing the tree to attach a terracotta pot is reminiscent of "When you find out your neighbours are Winemakers". It was a representation of the joy that can come from discovering a new hobby or tradition, especially when it involves alcohol.

From being given a new nickname to learning about traditional fermented drinks, I was constantly discovering new and exciting things about the world and the surrounding people.

Another incident that I often recall while reflecting on those days is tragic. It was a chaotic day at school when the children and teachers from the neighbouring local school came rushing to our school, seeking refuge. Apparently, one of their students had shot their teachers. Unfortunately, such incidents were not uncommon in the area, and the place was known for its tumultuous and erratic behaviour. Thankfully, things are now much improved, and we do not hear of such incidents in India anymore.

At school, I was an average performer academically and required extra assistance. I was lucky to have two dedicated teachers who would come after school hours to teach me. They were my saviours, especially in subjects like Chemistry, Physics, and Mathematics. In turn, they too would look forward to my mother's *fauji* hospitality. The Chemistry teacher, in particular, was a great foodie. He would wait patiently for my mother to serve him fresh snacks and a warm glass of milk before he would get down to teaching. My mother was an amazing cook, and her food was to die for. I think the Chemistry teacher would concur! This was one of the many quirky highlights of my school days.

I had a dear friend and classmate named Meenakshi who was my bestie. Her father, Col Mehta, was stationed with my father in Danapur. She was the epitome of grace and elegance, always dressed impeccably, and had a way with words that left an impression. It was through Meenakshi that I was introduced to the world of Mills and Boon, and the memories of our childhood adventures do not fail to enthral me even today.

However, life took us on different paths and Meenakshi migrated to Canada after our tenth grade. Time flew by and one fine day I received a letter from her after we reached college, but it was only after 35 years that we reconnected through Facebook. The memories of those teenage years flooded back, filled with secret crushes, discussions about who liked whom, and the endless pursuit of impressing our peers with our fashion choices. As we looked back on those times, we couldn't help but laugh at our youthful immaturity, a feeling that I'm sure many of us can relate to as we watch younger people around us from a newer generation go through similar experiences. The laughter and memories I shared with Meenakshi are like the comforting warmth of a summer sun, and even after all these years, our friendship continues to bloom like a wildflower.

And if I may add a touch of humour, when we look back at our secret crushes from so long ago, it's funny when we see the once young and handsome crushes now bald and aging, and we can't help but laugh along with them at the passage of time.

One evening, as I was settling down for the night, I received a surprise delivery of sandbags to place in front of my doors. Upon inquiring with my father, I was informed that there was a flood alert and all the drains in the area were running high, with the river water reaching dangerous levels and threatening to enter our neighbourhood. Although I don't have vivid memories of that event, I count the disaster management by the Army as one of life's small mercies.

Papa had extended an invitation to all our cousins (maternal and paternal) to visit him in Patna, and so, my uncles' children and my aunts' children, along with me, boarded a train from Delhi together. The passenger list included names such as Ganiv Chadha, Jyotan Chadha, Sovina Chadha, Amandeep Chadha, Guneet Chadha, and Mahip Chadha. During the journey, we were treated like VIPs and given preferential treatment, which we initially assumed was due to our large group size. Though, later that we realised the reason behind it - the railway staff had mistaken my father for a poor widower travelling with six children. The memory still makes me laugh.

In some cultures, extended family members are like an extended support system, always there to lend a hand. In others, family gatherings are like a reunion of old friends, filled with laughter, reminiscing, and making fresh memories. Regardless of how others perceived us, the bond that we shared as cousins will always be a cherished part of my life.

Danapur tenure also had in store, great news for us. As our two-year tenure approached its end and we were looking forward to another posting, papa received orders for his promotion to the rank of Colonel. While select grade Colonels are normally posted as Commanding Officers of Infantry Battalions as their first posting on approval, papa being a medical category was to assume a staff appointment, that of Administrative Commandant, Siliguri Military Station.

Siliguri Military Station was an amalgamation of many small pockets of military units located at Bagdogra, Bengdubi, Sukna and Siliguri. So, while papa's office was in Siliguri, we were allotted accommodation in the elephant-infested garrison of Bengdubi. These huge creatures would often come in hordes to stake their claim on the stocks of sugar and other rations stored in the local supply depot, an act which was accepted with respect (we had no choice!) After all, it was their natural abode and we the humans were the encroachers. I am told that to this day, the elephant-man relationship in Bengdubi and some other cantonments, like Narangi (Guwahati) remains unaltered.

Another interesting highlight of our stay in Bengdubi-Siliguri was the exciting shopping from across the border. In those days, the Indian markets had not opened, and the average Indian did not have easy access to imported crystalware, carpets, cosmetics, and even branded jeans and shoes. These needs could be fulfilled by undertaking a short 45-minute tempo drive, to a small but thriving market called Pani Tanki– near the border of Nepal. Everything exotic described above was available in plenty and cheap! Hence, a posting to Siliguri in those days was synonymous with sprucing up one's wardrobe if you were a teenager and for the mammas and papas, their homes! More so, mothers accumulate trousseau in the form of "Pink Lady dinner sets" or the famous exquisite golden cutlery.

Road tripping with papa, an army man bold,

To Darjeeling, Kalimpong, Gangtok we strolled,

With his tales of battles and maneuvers so grand,

Even traffic jams felt like a piece of cake in his hand!

This was also that crucial period in my student life when I had to decide on my higher education as I was soon to enter the 11th grade. Therefore, while my parents and Gini moved into their new home at Bagdogra, I would proceed westwards for my High School and later, graduation. It was time to fly away from the nest.

Crossroads Chandigarh –
1988 - 1993

After finishing my tenth grade in Danapur (Patna), I summoned the courage to make my parents aware of my desire to pursue the commerce stream. Unfortunately, my school displayed a lack of interest in offering commerce, much like a penguin's disinterest in desert hiking. In fact, the teachers sounded their annoyance loudly, saying, *"Kahe leeya first Division jub sciencewa nahein leena thaa?"* Meaning why take so much pain to get excellent results when you didn't want the science stream? But papa, the man with more connections than a spider's web, worked his magic and unearthed the treasure map to the land of commerce: Chandigarh. There was a slight catch, though - no hostels in sight. So, we settled on a proposal: I would stay with Amiji, that's my paternal grandma, folks! Alongside my dad's younger brother and his family in Chandigarh.

It was like a family reunion in the making, with a dash of educational ambition. It was also in a way for my father and our family to re-establish a bond with Chandigarh, a city he had left many decades ago when he moved to the academy to join the Army. As he had lost his father early, the family, originally from Srinagar in Kashmir, settled at a place which could provide stability to the young, widowed mother of three grown-up sons, both in terms of livelihood and quality education. That's when his grandfather helped them build 121 Sector 27A, a beautiful bungalow which oversaw not only the upbringing of these young boys but also the upbringing and growing up of the next generation – that is me and my immediate cousins.

So, there I was, standing on Amiji's doorstep, ready to embark on a turning point in my life. Amiji, the Mathematics and Punjabi wizard, was teaching in one of the finest schools in Chandigarh, St. John's. She was a force to be reckoned with. Despite facing adversity when she lost her husband early on, her determination only burned brighter. She had raised three champs: my dad (a military man), my uncle (a doctor), and another uncle (an engineer who rocked it at Asian Paints).

While I missed the love and affection of my own home, mummy's cuddles and mouthwatering delicacies, papa's imposing presence and the reassurance that came with it and last, but certainly not the least, my pranks, and niggles with Gini, life at Chandigarh was a nice, pleasant change. One learnt to adjust with the norms followed in another home, the rules of sharing, the independence of making one's own little decisions and above all, dealing on my own with small setbacks when things didn't go one's way - without mum or dad's comforting shoulders to lean on.

Yes, I did miss the sheltered *fauji* life of the military station. Notwithstanding, the first two years in my new school were a breeze, thanks to a military bus my dad arranged for me to travel to school. I had to hike fifteen minutes to the main road, but when that olive-green beauty rolled around the corner, I felt like royalty. This thirty-minute ride twice a day to school and back was also the incubator for many lifelong bonds – some of my most enduring friendships originated here. Today, three decades later and thousands of miles apart, bonds originated in this bus remain intact, alive and rocking – thanks to Rohit, Nipun, Khushdeep, Jagraj, Sartaj, Suchet, Rosey, Rubina and many more....

It was also a time to unleash my inner scholar and dabble in drama, declamation, and fine arts. I aced the school scene, thanks to my *fauji* upbringing that made adjusting a piece of cake. At home, my grandma ensured I had my cosy study nook, and my younger cousin became my partner in crime. We'd chat about our future escapades, walk and shop like there was no tomorrow, and generally have a good laugh.

My uncle, fondly addressed as "Doc" by his patients and friends, was my bus buddy on rainy days, erasing any hint of homesickness. He was also an avid golfer, and he'd often invite us to join him at the Chandigarh Golf Course, where he was a special, honourable member. Lunchtime at the golf course was a special treat. The smell of freshly cut grass and the sight of golfers in action were fascinating. We'd enjoy sumptuous meals together, relishing the food and each other's company. Those lunches were indeed the highlight of my otherwise busy week. And my aunt? Well, she was a senior professional at St. Kabir school. She found a mature friend in me. From going grocery shopping to our relationships to growing up and, of course, surviving in a joint family our evening chitchats covered everything! I secretly admired her for her seamless adjustments to our chaotic household.

Evenings in our joint family were a symphony of conversations and laughter. The dinner table was a place where we discussed our day, shared anecdotes, and sometimes engaged in friendly debates. My aunt, the family counsellor, was my go-to person for advice on life, relationships, and all the other challenges that came with growing up. She had a unique way of making everyone feel heard and understood. Our family friends, Anil and Singh uncle, were like modern days super buddies to my uncle. Upon their arrival, the house would transform into a space full of laughter and a livened-up atmosphere. Every family has friends and there are those whom you refer to as the inner circle. I connected with our inner circle outside the *fauji* eco system at Chandigarh.

Life was a never-ending learning journey, with our family as the teachers. Punjabi songs serenaded our kitchen escapades, and my grandma and her diabetes buddy went on daily marathon walks. In the evenings, we had a strict one-hour TV policy, and lights-out was like a military operation.

After acing twelfth grade, I joined Government College for Girls in Sector 42, which was 45 minutes away. Unfortunately, the Olive Green ride to the school was now outdated, and public transport options hardly existed in those days, leaving me struggling to reach my college on time. No sooner than he got a wink of my problem than super-dad swung into action! One sunny day, papa, who had been visiting Chandigarh, made a grand entrance on a red two-wheeler moped "Luna" to my pleasant surprise. I was a proud owner of a brand-new Luna, which was not only my new "college buddy" but also part of my identity. In those days, it cost less than a cup of coffee to fill up the tank, which would last an entire week and was enough to take me around the entire Chandigarh. The Luna served me, and later Gini, very well and provided me with a newfound independence as also the confidence to go wherever I wanted, whenever I wanted. As I drive my SUV today, I often recollect the humble beginnings that gave me the self-confidence to drive at  such an early age. With the Luna and a wardrobe full of new dresses, some crafted by Grandma, and others a delightful mix-and-match affair with my aunt and cousin, the navy blue and white uniform transformed into a riot of colours. I was ready to hit the new world at college.

Life in government college for girls was an exhilarating experience with this freshly gained independence. My friend Ritu, who had also joined the same course, became my confidante and support system. Her home became an extension of mine. She introduced me to the Rotary Club, turning me into a "Rotaractor." We attended seminars, meetings, and conferences, did some social good, and amped up our resumes.

Meanwhile, I finished college and graduated. Amiji, whom I admired was the biggest fan of her grandchildren, and always believed we would make her proud. She thought all her grandkids were destined for greatness, and her persuasive nature might have had something to do with it.

I wish to add here that there was this confusing time in college. Everyone was busy deciding on their future career choices. I was not far behind and even tried to apply for the first batch of the Indian Army Womens' Entry Scheme. Simultaneously, I also took an entrance exam for the cabin crew at Air India. A lesser-known fact is that I qualified for both.

My time away from my parents helped me develop self-confidence and a fighting spirit, which would serve me well in the future. Moving away from one's childhood home and living with a grandparent is a common experience in many cultures. From American sitcoms like "*The Golden Girls*" to the Indian film "*Dilwale Dulhania Le Jayenge,*" the theme of multigenerational families living together is universal and often brings out the best in people. Whether it's sharing meals, solving problems, or simply experiencing each other's company, these experiences help build strong family bonds that last a lifetime.

As we settled into our routine, one thing was obvious — every moment was a learning experience. Life in Chandigarh was about discovering the teacher in every family member. It was about understanding the value of togetherness, the strength of family bonds, and the joy of growing up surrounded by love and support. As I look back on those days in Chandigarh, I can't help but smile at the memories of family picnics to Timber Trail, Dakshai, Shimla, golf course lunches, and those unforgettable weekends in Chandigarh.

Those were the moments that shaped me and made me appreciate the beauty of life with the extended family, beyond the comfort zone of one's ecosystem. This place equipped me with the skills to be independent and ready to tackle whatever life threw my way. My time over here was filled with recollections. Friends I made there have stayed connected with me. My friends from high school have reconnected with me after a span of Thirty-two years. Sartaj, Shamsher, Rajeshwar, Gauri, Neeti, Bipin, Palwinder, Neelakshi, Jagraj, Darshan Chander, Dayena, Sangeeta, Khushdeep, and Jaspreet… to name a few. Remembering the aftermath of the Mandal Commission Report, visiting my parents who had moved to Bathinda during this period, gathering experiences of staying in a joint family, and riding my red two-wheeler scooter with the tag line "*Chal Meri Luna*" playing in the background.

Reflecting on those times, I can now laugh at the memoirs and the naivety of my younger self, again emphasising the changes in outlook and appearances of old school friends. But I am grateful for the experiences and the people who made those years so special.

A New Course of Life – via Bathinda, 1993

During this period, my parents received their next posting order. This time they were to move closer to home, to a place called Bathinda (Punjab). It is in the northwestern part of the country, about four hours away from Chandigarh. My sister, grandmother, and I were visiting my parents in Siliguri when papa got his transfer orders to Punjab. Gini and I left on the train with my grandmother while my parents decided to travel by car along with our pet, Pedro the Dachshund.

It was a long drive across the breadth of the country and had to be made in our Ambassador, a far cry from the comfortable and efficient cars of today. But he, being the incorrigible adventurer, pooh-poohed all suggestions and advice against the idea and unilaterally dismissed them. As luck would have it, just on the outskirts of Banaras, their car met with an accident. The car was written off as a total loss. While mummy was completely unhurt, papa survived miraculously with a fracture on his leg. My father was evacuated to the nearest military hospital in Lucknow. The wreckage of the car was sold as a scrap. Thereafter, mummy moved headed for Delhi by train. As the doorbell rang in the wee hours of the morning, Gini and I rushed to open the gate to let the car in. But alas, we couldn't see any but we saw mummy, Pedro and our maid and her son at the gate. We were shocked at listening to her narrative. While I was already well entrenched in Chandigarh by then, Gini still had to join college. So, when papa recovered, they all moved together to Bathinda.

While in Chandigarh, I regularly visited Bhatinda on my weekends. During one of my visits, Mummy was, suspiciously, extra nice to me and the extra dose of pampering was palpable. It turned out she wanted me to meet a young Captain (Sheri) who was coming over to his Commanding Officers' place. Unknown to me, an unspoken arrangement had already taken place between the Brigade Commander (Brig. P.K Saighal), Commanding Officer (Col. Shivaji Chakravarty), his wife, and my parents. They had exchanged pictures. My to-be fiancé and I were set up in the garb of an invitation where we were to have the privilege of joining my parents for an evening at the home of his Commanding Officer.

I was completely taken aback when I found out about this coordinated meeting. It was like being transported back in time to an era when arranged marriages were the norm and a modern Chandigarh girl. Nonetheless, despite my instinctive rebellious response to the proposition, I must admit that there was a tinge of mysterious excitement.

I was nervous and anxious as the day of the arranged meeting approached. It was a feeling that I imagine was not too dissimilar to what people in ancient times must have felt when they went to meet their potential spouse for the first time. Back then, arranged marriages were the norm, but in modern times, the idea of being set up with someone was a bit foreign to me. However, there was also a sense of enigmatic anticipation that came with it. In a way, it was also quite thrilling to think about the prospect of meeting someone who could potentially become my life partner. My nerves started getting the better of me. Would we hit it off? The unknown was both exhilarating and nerve-racking. But, as luck would have it, everything just seemed to fall into place. The young Captain pleasantly surprised me when I met him that day. As we took our conversation forward, I could feel myself relaxing.

As the evening progressed, my to-be fiancé (Sheri) and I found ourselves in a scintillating conversation with each other. Our exchange covered the quirky similarities between our families and the humorous incidents that had taken place in our lives. Our tête-à-tête had us so immersed in each other that time just flew by, and it was well past dinner time. While other invitees were waiting at the dinner table, our conversation did not seem to see any ending in sight – everyone around us was eager to know what we were talking about.

After a while, we bid each other good night, uncertain whether we would meet again, each circumspect about the other's true feelings. Little did I know that the impact of our conversation was so great that he couldn't wait to share it with his parents. Sheri later divulged that as soon as we had said our goodbyes, he had immediately called them to give them a rundown of the amazing time he had spent talking to me. It was a delightful evening filled with laughter, intriguing meeting, and a newfound appreciation for an upbringing in a different household. I wondered if our paths might cross again in the future, and who knew, perhaps we would have another engaging conversation to add to the memories of that night. Little did I know that there would be an intention of my parents of inviting his family over.

That first meeting was quite like a scene from a romantic movie - a modern take on the classic fairytale, with the parents acting as the fairy godparents, setting us up on a path toward a potential happily ever after. It was a new experience for me, as it turned out to be a defining moment in my life.

It is another story though, as to how this meeting took place in the first place; nothing short of a truly divine intervention. In those days, it was widespread practice for the bachelor's to impromptu call on (read self-invite and raid) the Commanding Officers' (CO) residence, particularly when they felt the temperatures rising at the workplace.

Having caught the CO and the first lady off guard, it would help let out some steam and notionally settle scores. This was one of those evenings, however, with a twist. As the youngsters in their buoyant mood were going through the final adieu rituals, the CO's wife put an envelope and put it in Sheri's front pocket. Being an eligible bachelor, much in demand, he could easily guess the contents without even opening it. He knew it would contain a prospective bride's picture. However, the Alpha inflated ego had decided that the envelope would not be opened. How could the first lady decide on a life partner for him? So off went the envelope to the confines of his dresser, with no intention of ever being opened.

A few days later, a hockey contingent was visiting the formation for a tournament, and the officers were supposed to share their rooms. Lt. (later Col) Sajan Mohideen was assigned to Sheri's room and while Sheri was away at the office, he noticed the buddy dusting and fiddling with the envelope…. Curiosity getting the better of him, he opened the forbidden envelope and on finding a picture of a beautiful lass, adorned it with flowers and gave it a place of honour on the dressing table! Sajan was all smiles during lunch that day and when his curiosity had had enough of him, he asked Sheri who the woman in the picture was. Sheri had no option but to see the picture and that was when a chord struck…like it always does in the Hindi movies – as they say, "They lived happily after"! We often give credit to Sajan and the buddy for connecting us. Had they not noticed the photo, it would have never come out of the envelope or the closet!

A few years later, Sheri shared another hilarious encounter involving one of his seniors, the one and only Niroop Chandran, something that occurred only a few months before our engagement. Niroop had this assignment to visit the higher headquarters along with Sheri – you know, where all the serious stuff happens. And, as luck would have it, he crossed paths with my father. Imagine this: Niroop, all serious and official, meets my father, who's like a walking mountain with a personality that could charm unicorns. Niroop, with a grin that could rival a comedian's, says to Sheri, "Check out your future!" Yep, he was pointing at my father's imposing presence, predicting a future of health, wealth, and wisdom.

But hold on for the plot twist. Little did they know, this chance meeting was more than just a quip. Niroop's prophetic words turned into a cosmic joke. Sheri grew into a pillar of health – chasing calories, right? Wealthy? In laughter and priceless experiences. Wiser? Well, let's just say a plethora of life-enriching experiences. So, hats off to Niroop. His playful remark turned into a prediction that's now a legendary tale of laughter and irony.

Rewind to Diwali (this was just before I met Sheri), the Indian festival of lights is normally celebrated in October or November every year. It is believed that the Goddess of wealth and prosperity blesses you on this occasion. A group of officers while making their rounds to different regimental officers' houses to raise a toast, as was the tradition those days, coincidentally landed up at the unearthly hour of 1:00 a.m. on the first floor of our block where one of their unit families lived. Already happy with the effect of imbibing different whiskies and a mix of rum and beer too, one of them had the dubiously brilliant idea of lighting a sparkler and throwing it from the first floor into our courtyard.

He didn't realise that it had aggravated our pet dog on the ground floor. The dog ended up biting my sister. My father, being the strict disciplinarian he was, shouted at the top of his lungs and made the officers line up. As the last sparkler fizzled out behind his back, so did the effect of the fine liquor in their heads, I can only imagine how relieved those poor officers must have felt to have dodged a bullet!

That Diwali was indeed memorable for reasons more than one. Earlier that auspicious evening, a very touching episode took place. Just before this group of youngsters had disturbed the peace of our block, we as a family had just seen off two young officers after a nice, pleasant dinner.

A special train (Soldiers' Movement Train), as per norm, led by an Officer Commanding and his second in command, was passing through Bathinda. The train was transporting the 7th Battalion of the GARHWAL Rifles to its new duty station and was temporarily halted at Bathinda Station that night, and those days such an overnight halt meant a dull Diwali sans family and celebrations. My parents loved playing host and that evening it was destined that these two officers on duty aboard the military special train were to join us.

One of them was Capt. Baljeet, who was papa's coursemate's son, and with him, was Maj. Cherish Mathson, his senior, in the battalion. Being aware of papa's posting in Bathinda, he suggested the idea of surprising us, to which the Major was initially hesitant due to his lack of personal acquaintance with the family and his reluctance to intrude upon the festivities. Notwithstanding, Baljeet convinced him, and what followed was a lovely evening over excellent wine and food with lots of '*fauji kissas,*' reminiscences, and anecdotes.

The young Major expressed his gratitude through a DO (Demi-Official Letter) to my dad a week later conveying his feelings and I quote, "Though a Christian by religion, 12 years in the army has made Diwali very much a festival I look forward to. The bleak prospect of spending a Diwali evening suffering a mosquito bite in a halted train at Bathinda railway station was miraculously transformed into a memorable evening, thanks to your wonderful hospitality and instant acceptance of a person just introduced to you. I cannot forget the warmth and affection which flowed so spontaneously. Please convey my warm regards and profuse thanks to Mrs Chadha & and your daughters for their hospitality" .... While Cherish Mathson graciously conveyed his feelings through the DO, how much it meant to my military man father was revealed only 25 years later when I discovered the handwritten letter preserved neatly among his cherished documents, long after he was no more and the young Major had risen to be an Army Commander, one of the top eight Generals of the Indian Army- Military traditions, bonds and chivalry at their very best.

It's amazing to think about how seemingly trivial moments like the Diwali celebration, chance meeting at the Headquarters and other preceding chain of events ended up bringing Sheri, me, and our families into each other's lives and eventually leading to our arranged marriage. It just goes to show that you never know what life has in store for you. Looking back, I'm also convinced that some cosmic force was controlling my transition from a brat to a spouse – all within the *fauj* so dear to me!

PART II

MARCHING

FORWARD —

WEDDING BELLS

LOVE, LAUGHTER,

& LIVELY

ADVENTURES

In our cozy abode, a humble little space,
with friends by my side, life's joys embrace.
No riches to boast about, just laughter and cheer,
small happiness reigns, making each day dear.

The Patiala Peg:
"Cheers From Patiala"

Being married to a defence officer was the path I chose during my final college years. Despite the many perks of civilian life my relations tried to show me – a stable existence, coupled with monetary benefits, and permanency in career and family – the latent adventurer in me couldn't bring itself to settle down at one place, a monotonous routine, and the so-called stable life. Despite the seemingly unsettled nomadic life, I adored my father's profession, associated community living and the exciting flavours it brought along. I had seen my grandparents experience it in another era and my mother in her role as an army spouse was my ultimate role model. Yes, for me *'fauj'* definitely scored over 'Civil'! and the golden period of courtship was about to begin.

As a young girl smitten with love, I spent many hours on the phone chatting with my crush, Sheri, who was the Adjutant (the right-hand man of the Commanding Officer) of his regiment. Although he was a busy man, always on call with his boss, he always made time for me, even if his responses were short and sweet. One night, my father caught me talking on the official *fauji* phone in the storeroom, the instrument having travelled throughout the house. The next morning, I woke up to find that an additional telephone connection had been set up in my room, making our conversations even easier.

In the evenings, Sheri and I would spend time together at different venues within and outside the cantonment, be it the parks, rose garden, local restaurants, or the open-air cinema, perhaps made just for us (so I felt, those days!). As an Adjutant, Sheri had been told to always keep his memo pad and pen with him and to always be near a telephone line, just in case his boss needed him. Throughout our courtship, I was completely oblivious that the sweet nothings exchanged between Sheri and me were often witnessed by our friends and family, who were all enjoying themselves. Moreover, when Sheri was on leave in Patiala for a few days, I had to even go through two telephone exchanges to reach him. But it was all worth it to be able to connect with the love of my life.

As I reminisce on our story, I can't help but think of how different our experience would have been in other cultures. For example, in some parts of our country, arranged marriages were strict and there was no room for a romantic courtship like ours. It allowed us to savour the freedom and love.

I constantly compared us on our never-ending phone chats to the characters in "You've Got Mail" or made jokes about the lengths to which I would go for a delightful conversation with Sheri. Love in the modern age can be quite a ride, but I wouldn't have it any other way. Our courtship lasted for four months, and the military exchange must have felt relieved when we finally got married, knowing that the busy phone lines would soon become freer.

Days became months and our parents decided it was time we got engaged. Excited about this next step in our relationship, I decided to do my trousseau shopping in Patiala, a place famous for its royal embroidery and where Sheri's parents lived. Sheri's mom also thought that it would be best for me to do my shopping myself. I was originally scheduled to stay there for only two days, but little did I know that there was an extended stay in store, another cosmic intervention, to expedite strengthening of bonds with my new especially my would-be mom-in-love.

Because of unexpected and severe rains in the area, something which was not normal in Patiala, my stay was extended to ten days amidst heavy flooding, without electricity and running water. The year 1993 was particularly devastating for the state of Punjab, causing the railways and land transport to come to a complete halt.

During this extended stay in Patiala, I was constantly worried about the well-being of my family and friends back home. My fiancé Sheri, on the other hand, was equally worried about us and asked his friend, Khalid, posted at Patiala to look us up. Khalid's unit, stationed at Patiala, was requisitioned and deployed on flood relief duties and allocated air effort for reconnaissance and surveillance of the affected areas. On the designated day, Khalid, like a maverick, decided to route the aerial survey to cover our colony. Thus, one day, as I was gazing out of the window, I noticed a helicopter circling overhead. My initial thought was that it was part of a regular aerial survey of the area.

Little did I know the helicopter was on the most important hi priority mission on the request of a coursemate to check the well-being of the family, particularly the "damsel in distress" (that's me!).

As it turned out, my fiancé friend had been so worried about my safety that he felt compelled to come and check on us on the ground, too. His gesture touched me deeply and remains a testament to the strong bonds of friendship and concern that we share even after so many years. I will never forget the thrill of being checked upon by a helicopter, especially during a time of such extreme weather conditions. It is a moment that I will cherish forever, and it will always serve as a reminder of the kindness and care that my fiancé's friends and family have shown me.

Floods were soon over, and it was time for the rituals to commence; the first one being the 'Roka' cum engagement. The engagement ritual conducted in the Officers' Mess turned out to be a unique fun event. With my fiancé's unit officers and coursemates in attendance from the groom's side and my father's colleagues representing the bride's family, the ceremony was more of a *fauji* get together very much intriguing for our respective relatives, who were a minority not only in strength but also in activity. As far as uniqueness was concerned, that was not all. In normal circumstances, as per traditions, the function is to be hosted by the bride's family while the groom and his family are welcomed as guests. Thanks, once again, to recurring cosmic intervention, the absolute reverse happened. Because of the delay in my return caused by floods at Patiala, I (the bride) accompanied my in-laws as the guest of honour to the venue, while hubby dear was busy toiling hard making arrangements in the Officers' Mess along with my father as the perfect host – small perks of marrying a junior officer posted in the same station where your father-in-law is a senior in the higher headquarters!

With the ring ceremony done and dusted, the focus shifted to the wedding and customary honeymoon plans. Those days, our salaries did not permit destination weddings and foreign trips were unheard of. Hence, one had to be content with our desi salubrious destinations. Fortunately for us, Sheri had been nominated to attend the very sought-after D&M (whatever that means!) Course at Bengaluru (Bangalore) soon after the wedding date, a perfect opportunity for us to enjoy an extended honeymoon at the Pub and Disco capital of India.

Sheri's Commanding Officer, however, had different ideas. Being a career course and wanting him to study and perform well, he felt I would be a distraction and asked him to go alone. This was like an unpleasant '*Akbar ka farmaan*' (Akbar's diktat)!

In the Indian Army, the official age for getting married is 25 years, and if an officer wished to get married before that age, he needed to make a written request to the Commanding Officer who would grant permission under exceptional circumstances. Without this permission, no government accommodation would be provided for the newly married couple. We both knew that we fell into this tricky category and didn't want to risk acting against the wishes of the boss!

However, as luck would have it, the Commanding Officer himself had initiated tying our destinies and was keen that we hit the altar ASAP. This ensured we were in the safe zone. Sheri, not the one to be deterred by such '*farmaans,*' was determined to make his boss agree to his terms and replied, "I will proceed with the course and take my wife, Gonu, with me. If that is not possible, sir, then we will get married after I complete the course." To everyone's surprise, the Commanding Officer had no choice but to agree to Sheri's request.

I couldn't help but admire my fiancé's determination and strong-willed attitude. Despite facing opposition, he stood his ground and made sure that our plans of mixing business with pleasure remained intact. This is a testament to the love and commitment he has for me and our relationship.

Our wedding day was set for October 16th, 1993, and the preparations were in full swing.

My father took on the task of planning the guests' stay, coordinating events, and making sure everything was perfect. On the other side, my mother-in-law was the event coordinator, making sure that every moment was in sync and went smoothly. The bride's guests were accommodated in neighbouring guest rooms, while the groom's guests and relatives were put up in a hotel. We didn't want to take any chances and made sure that everyone was able to attend the wedding. ON TIME!

And let's not forget the funny meme references we could make - like comparing the wedding planning process to the chaos of "The Hangover" or joking about how my father was the ultimate "wedding planner" long before the term even existed.

But despite the challenges and differences, the love and excitement of the day overshadowed everything else. Our wedding day was the start of our forever, and I wouldn't have wanted it any other way.

The day of the wedding finally arrived, and it was a bustling one. On the evening before the wedding, we had planned a sangeet ceremony - an evening of dance, music, and dinner. The bride's father had transformed into a DJ for the night and entertained us with foot-tapping numbers. It was an evening that would be remembered for years to come, as everyone, including the groom, was seen dancing to the beat of the music. Both sides being *faujis*, the entire station, including the Corps Commander was on the guest list. While the officers from Sheri's unit constituted the power-packed '*Baraatis*' on the dance floor, Team 'Second Thud' led by the Commanding Officer, Col Balbir Pama stole everyone's hearts when they showed up all in formal 6B ceremonial Mess Dress the way from Lalgarh Jattan (about 200 km from Bathinda) to play the perfect hosts in solidarity with the bride's dad. So much to the bonhomie and camaraderie of the Gurkhas!

The next morning was filled with excitement and a flurry of last-minute preparations. The groom was made to sit on a horse, a traditional practice in many cultures, 100 meters away from the '*Gurudwara*' (Sikh temple). Rohini, his sister, made the horse eat gram dal soaked overnight, while his eldest brother's wife put *kajal* (a cosmetic powder used to darken the eyes) in the groom's eyes. It was a comical scene, and we couldn't help but laugh at the groom's discomfort at getting married in the same station where he was posted and serving his tenure.

Finally, the baraat, the procession of the groom's family and friends, reached the temple after a five-minute ride, much to the groom's relief. Despite being embarrassed because of the feeling of being under the glare of his own troops, coupled with the discomfort of unfamiliar wedding rituals, he put on a supporting show and obliged. It was a beautiful wedding, and a day filled with joy, laughter, and new beginnings.

The ceremony was emotional and joyous for everyone involved. The rituals of the Sikh wedding, including the encircling of the holy book, had a significance that touched the hearts of all those present. During each circle, the priest would recite the holy scriptures, and we would bow down in reverence.

This was a new experience for my husband, who was more used to military traditions, than to traditional Indian weddings. He was surrounded by his entire regiment, all dressed in their best ceremonial attire, watching with awe as the wedding ceremony took just over half an hour to complete. Later, 1 comprehended, that while conducting a very private function in the full glare of the Regiment and its personnel seemed embarrassing at that time, this event helped in cementing our bonds with the troops in the long run. Even today, long after having left the unit in 2005, and my husband having commanded another Regiment, the troops of '28 *Thambi Tigers*' still relate to me as the young bride who was welcomed into the Regiment so intimately – intangibles of *fauji* life which cannot be replicated elsewhere!

At Indian weddings, there is a fun and light-hearted tradition of hiding the groom's shoes and other belongings, which are typically taken by the bride's sisters. After the ceremony is over, they playfully ask for a price to return them. As I stepped out to change into another outfit, my sisters and cousins were quick to make the most of this opportunity, and my husband's wallet soon found itself in their hands. This playful ritual added a touch of humour to the otherwise solemn occasion and is a reminder of the light-heartedness that is often present in traditional Indian weddings.

As I settled into the car after lunch, I couldn't help but feel a mix of excitement and nervousness. I was starting my new life as a married woman, but I was also leaving my childhood home behind. However, I was happy knowing that my parents would be there, in the same colony- just a stone's throw away, for me whenever I needed them.

After the wedding, we made our way to Patiala, once the well-known royal state of Punjab. Dubbed the "city of palaces, gardens, and Polo and not to forget the legendary peg!", Patiala was a new adventure waiting to happen.

Upon arriving at my husband's home in Patiala, we indulged in a ritual where the groom had to stop his mother from drinking water at least five times. It was a fun thing and after this, he made his mother drink water. I was just around 38 kilos back then, and all of Sheri's sisters were blocking the doorway as they told their brother that he would have to carry me all the way to enter the living room. Sheri just jumped at the offer and picked me up, carrying me into the house…oops, I dare him, we can't do this anymore…ha ha ha! This was just the beginning of the warm welcome I received from my new relatives, who showered me with gifts. At one point in time, all I could see their shoes more than their faces, as I had touched over twenty-five pairs of feet at my "*Muh Dikhayee,*" a tradition where the bride is welcomed in the new home with presents and gifts.

After the wedding, my husband and I were treated to a dinner hosted by his parents for his guests and their friends. The festivities were a celebration of our union and a chance to spend time with our loved ones. In total contrast to the 'Sangeet' party at Bathinda Officers' Institute, this was a function organised and celebrated in a traditional Punjabi way, with *Patialvi* hospitality at its best. We were truly blessed to have amongst us, besides other local guests, the entire young crowd from *"Twenty-Eight'* as well as Sheri's coursemates and class fellows from RIMC arriving from far away locations of their postings, Siachen glacier included! No wonder, all of them, Deepak, Vikram, Saby, NC, JS, Bibhor, Ravi, Amit and many more, remain part of our inner circle to this day; truly blessed to have them part of our lives.

The celebrations were not over yet. We decided to take a romantic getaway to McLeodganj, also known as "little Lhasa," in Dharamshala, where we could relax and unwind in the beautiful hills of Kangra District. The trip was a beautiful and memorable experience, and after a few days, we made our way back to our place of work in Bhatinda.

The Newly Commissioned Bride!

As we returned from our vacation to Bathinda, we were greeted by an extended family (our regiment) who were more than eager to welcome us. I had the rare joy of participating in the many traditions that come with it.

One of these traditions was a dining-in evening, where my husband's colleagues went above and beyond to make our arrival special.

Upon our reaching the station, we stayed at my parent's place, in the Officers' Colony, which was a good 8-9 kms from the unit's Officers' Mess. We were told to be ready by the designated time, and a suitable transport would be deputed to pick us up.

The doorbell rang bang on time. There were six young bachelors led by the senior-most, Capt. Roopam standing outside, ready to escort us  on their gleaming new motorcycles. And imagine my surprise when I saw our ride – an amazingly decorated and lit up cycle rikshaw.

The joyful memory of being piloted on this unique transport all the way to the unit cutting across the entire Bathinda Cantt, a novel way to welcome a new family member to the '*Twenty-Eight*' family, is still vivid and brings a smile to my lips whenever I reflect on it. As we left our home, we were cheered on by my parents' enamoured neighbours who had seen nothing like this. The evening to follow was an equally cherished one, and I still think back on it with fondness recollecting the '*Greh Parvesh*' (Traditional way of welcoming the new bride) performed by the senior ladies in the unit, led by the charming and affectionate Mrs Negi. In that year we were to witness a series of such weddings and unique welcome ceremonies in the regiment as Upi, Shaswati, Shivali and Ritu joined us one by one, each one of them being greeted in a different but exciting manner, be it on a decorated bullock cart or the trailer of a military truck with the military band in attendance inside the truck.

As I reflect on this special time in my life, I realise that in some backgrounds, the bride and groom go on a honeymoon right after the wedding, while in others, the couple spends time with their families before setting off on their journey together. I had the best of both the worlds, in fact more than our legitimate share, as we had more than one family to welcome me into their folds.

Overall, it was a wonderful start to my new life as a married woman and a member of the Armed Forces fraternity, this time as a '*Bahu*' – a transition from the '*Beti*'! Imagine my status change – the children of officers who were common acquaintances of my father and my husband, suddenly, and for some strange reason began to address me as 'aunty' while all this while I had been a '*Didi*'!

As a newly married woman, there was one thing that I was completely unprepared for; i.e, cooking. I had never been in the kitchen and didn't know the first thing about making a meal. I voiced my concerns to my husband, who then spoke to his mother. She calmly told me that while we could eat out for five days a week, eventually my husband's salary would run out and home cooking and starting my kitchen was inevitable and the only option.

At first, I was intimidated by the thought of being responsible for feeding us, but Kiran was in the neighbourhood to help me. Our houses were conveniently located just a stone's throw away from each other, and as soon as my husband left for work, I would run over to my mother's house. There, she would pamper me by oiling my hair, and I would relax. Time would fly and soon it would be time for Sheri's return from the office – triggering panic with the realisation that lunch was not ready! Kiran, the ever-doting mother, would quickly pack lunch for us, reminding me to take it out of her utensils and swap it with mine. This was her subtle way of reminding me of her instructions and making sure that I was learning the ropes of cooking – as also managing my new married life.

I took the advice to heart, but let's just say, my cooking skills were…definitely lacking.

My younger sister, Gini, who was in college at the time, happened to be a natural chef – alas there was no Master Chef

India in those days, else she would have been a celebrity by now. She would frequently stop by to check in on my progress and always try to encourage and guide me, but the bitter truth was that my portions and measurements needed a lot of work. Despite her best efforts to help, I would often serve up meals that were, shall we say, less than impressive. This would always lead to a good-natured laugh between us, with Gini teasing me about my culinary expertise (in fact, the opposite of that!). It so happened that once she ventured into my kitchen and decided to taste my preparation, not realising that she had gobbled up the entire portion until I shrieked it was all my lunch. Her face was a study in disbelief as she commented, 'You are impossible sister...you better increase your measurements and portions...' Having said that, she quickly whipped up a sumptuous meal for both of us. Gini was indeed an expert chef right from the beginning.

Yes, it was all genuine fun, and I knew my sister was always there to support me. Apart from my sister, there was another one young lady in the Regiment with whom I could relate comfortably and confide my real-world problems. She was Mrs Upi Dewan, who stayed close to our home and had been married earlier that year. She was instrumental in guiding me through the finer nuances of '*Ghar Ghirasti*,' despite being from a nonmilitary background. She still had the best articulatory and soothing guidance to share whenever I required. Soon the ladies from our regiment, Mrs Neeraj Bakshi, Damyanti Negi, Simple Sahay, Jyoti Gurung, Jyoti Dhillon, Shashwati Rudra later Sayali Kekre and Shivali

Ranaut, to name a few, became my guiding mentors – and more than that close reassuring friends.

It was these small moments that made the transition into married life much easier, and I will always cherish them.

Just like a recruit is considered trained once he clears his drill or PT tests, I was given to believe that the litmus test of a new *fauji* bride is the successful hosting of a dinner for the Commanding Officer. My day of reckoning arrived. Sheri subtly told me that we were to host a dinner at home. His Commanding Officer would come along with some other selected officers and their wives. The realisation soon dawned upon me that If I didn't think of something quickly, the whole truth of my sub-optimal culinary abilities would soon be out in the open. But in Hindi, there is a proverb – *'doobte ko tinke ka sahara'* A drowning person will find help in a twig too. I rushed to my savior, my mom. So Chandbir Daju (elder brother in Nepalese) was sent as the man in shining armor. He announced, *'Didi maa aa gayaa teme phikar na garnus'* (Sister, I have arrived, don't worry). In a few minutes, my dinner comprising a king's menu of lentils, rice, chicken, curd, salad, rotis, and vegetables was ready. He even gave me quick and ready instructions on a suitable way of presentation for the dinner party after heating. I followed them to the hilt, and we were ready to host our first party as a couple – the excitement and anxiety were culpable. The guests arrived, and we did our best to play the perfect hosts. The evening flowed on with an abundance of fun, gossip and laughter, as did the snacks and Solan No1 & Old Monk, the popular brands of liquor those days. It was soon time for dinner to be served.

While I was in the kitchen preparing to lay the table, one of the guest's wives entered the kitchen and asked if she could help. And she saw me panicking, having realised that the desert had been left out! As I confided in her that I had forgotten to prepare the sweet dish. She looked at me reassuringly and asked me if I had some flour and custard. I gave them to her and in no time; she produced a trifle pudding. She told me to promise her that I would take all the credit for the sweet and not even tell my husband. I still have the highest regard for Mrs Negi! I cannot forget to mention the mushy laudatory and proud looks from my husband, who thought I had turned into a chef *par excellence!* I also said to myself, "Fake it till you make it" as I took all the credit for the delicious trifle pudding, even though I did not know how to make it myself. Little did I know what was going to happen next.

The night was a complete success, and my husband and I felt like we had aced the role of playing hosts perfectly as another step in our journey as a couple. That was reinforced the next day when my husband's Commanding Officer called to compliment us on the dinner. My heart sank as I realised, I had to come clean about the sweet dish, which I did sheepishly, but to my pleasant surprise, Sheri just hugged me and called up Mrs Negi to thank her.

The practice of hosting our comrades, friends, seniors, and family in our homes is a global custom to commemorate various occasions, be it a housewarming, thanksgiving, welcoming someone to a new place, or accommodating those who are newly stationed or just passing through. While the meal shared during these gatherings need not be extravagant, its simplicity signifies the profound intention of extending a heartfelt welcome to those new to our organisation or gratitude towards those we love and respect.

Such incidents, which were quite frequent, became a source of laughter and joy in our extended family, and we still reminisce about them to this day. It's moments like these that make life's journey a little sweeter, like a warm and comforting trifle pudding. Personally, I couldn't have asked for a better start on my journey as a new bride and hostess.

Bedding In:
A Tale Of Two Cities
Bangalore & Gopalpur –
1994

T he course at the Army School of Mechanical Transport had already been assigned to Sheri, who was more than eager to leave Bathinda and proceed to Bangalore. We packed our motorbike and took it along, a decision which would prove worth a million dollars!

As we reached the institution which to our joy was located right in the heart of the city, a small two-room accommodation was allotted to us. For me, it was a newfound (and well deserved too!) freedom. No breakfast was to be prepared, lunch was in the Mess, and dinners were dedicated to exploring the fine dining joints in the city. Life was indeed fun, and we made the most of our extended honeymoon. As a lazy and unenthusiastic cook, I was delighted with the routine. Well, that was all that a newly married lady could ask for. Far from the madding crowd, being woken up with breakfast in bed to start the days and candlelight dinners to end them, I savoured this preferential treatment for three months.

Young officers, most of them newly married, were present on the course and that made us mostly a group of young girls from all around the country and different Regiments with one thing in common – all of us were looking for our feet as army spouses and at the same time looking for friendship and fun. What an interesting course, I thought to myself. As soon as the husbands would leave for their classes, the ladies would gather to discuss alternative places to explore, and where to tickle tastebuds. The local cafeteria was our usual rendezvous and after a lazy breakfast, usually in our own rooms, we would gather there for coffee and, of course, gossip! Usually, we were careful enough to behave decently and ladylike as also vacate the premises around the time for our husbands' mid-day tea and snacks break.

However, there were a few occasions when exciting gossip got the better of us and the DS Coord had to order us out as our shrieks and laughter threatened to cross the red lines of decorum expected! Well, 'girls too just wanna have some fun' even though they are now ladies! There were days when we even ventured out shopping and exploring the city. Bangalore being famous for silk, sandalwood and a lot of other traditional stuff besides being the fashion capital of India those days.

During the midterm break, we all planned a bike ride to Mysore and Ooty, nearby tourist attractions. While Sheri and I, all excited, packed and our fuel tank topped up, were raring to go, our friends somehow backed out. Not the ones to be disappointed. We dared it on our own; I use the term dared, as it was Veerappan territory in those days. That bike trip proved to be one of the most adventurous and fulfilling ones and, the kick starts of many such couple road trips in the years to come!

Course life was indeed lots of fun, despite the demanding work required to be put in by the officers who were continuously bombarded with challenging assignments and exams by the faculty. The quest to make the most of the break, away from usual unit routine, especially for those whose units were in field areas or even remote Class B cities/ towns. There were pubs and cafes to explore, live concerts to attend, make the most of the popular Ranjit Singhji Institute located bang on MG Road and above all, numerous get-togethers with coursemates and new friends acquired during this training assignment. While I had heard so much about this 'coursemate bonding' from my dad too, it was here that I experienced and fell in love with it—no doubt camaraderie and friendship in the Services transcends all other forms of human-caused barriers, sometimes surpassing even family bonds. I could now relate to that famous quote by Richard Bach: "The bond that links your true family is not one of blood, but of respect and joy in each other's life. Rarely do members of one family grow up under the same roof."

Sheri was enamoured to see me adjusting as his better half and befriending his friends effortlessly. On his part, he took on the task of quietly, but surely, equipping me to manage all scenarios, which, of course, I was partly already familiar with as an army man's daughter. But as I moved along, I soon realised that the experience of an army kid wasn't enough. Besides grooming his lady love, he gave me all the required empathy to become a strong, resilient woman.

But as they say, there are no free lunches. In return, I wrote his Thesis Project (complete submission by hand, keeping in mind the minor Staff Duties) since laptops were unheard of, and helped him learn his lessons. "We" were adjudged as the best student on the campus. So ultimately disproving the revered Commanding Officers' hypothesis that young wives can only be distracting. I can state with pride that wives are not only fun but incentives for doing well!!

Coming back to the girls – I refer to them as girls because we were all in the age group of 21 to 24 years on the course. We became friends with no benefits, pure simple friendship. Soon, I suddenly realised, from among our group, one young lady began missing our girlie adventures, so I was tasked with finding out why. It turned out that she was on the family way, soon going to have a baby. While she was thrilled to announce it to me, she was also apprehensive about broadcasting the news to all and sundry. I understood the need for me to remain quiet and 'mum' was the word. But we shared a unique bond and spent a lot of time together, me offering a comforting shoulder in her tough days and, in turn, gaining firsthand experience of how to deal with pre-motherhood grinds.

The course was soon over, and we parted ways.

I soon learned that my friend gave birth to a baby girl and named her Ganiv. Ahhhh… so adorable to have someone named after you. Due to our different paths, we lost touch – there was no Facebook or WhatsApp in those days! After many years, almost two decades later, we had a chance encounter when they updated me with the good news of little Ganiv, who had grown up into a smart young lady lawyer and had just been commissioned as an officer in the Armed Forces. Life indeed comes full circle. I'm sure somewhere my latent desire to adorn the uniform was fulfilled by Captain Ganiv.

We were soon back to Bathinda and, more importantly, back to unit routine (read Mother Earth!). For Sheri, it was return to the Adjutant's chair, which for me appeared to have an extraordinary gravitational pull that ensured time spent outside the unit area was minimal. For me, it was back to household chores, something I continued to struggle with. As a couple, we were faced with a unique problem, something of our own making. Sheri wasn't 25 yet and hence, as per military rules, not entitled to family accommodation! So, it was a nomadic existence, waiting for a married couple to go on long leave or course so that we could move into their house. Notwithstanding, thanks to military brotherhood and bonhomie, there were many volunteers. The Army indeed has its own solutions to peculiar problems, unique to the military rules and way of life. In this regard, we remain ever grateful to Roopam and Shaswati for the time we spent in their lovely nest, the first home to both couples – them and us.

In this backdrop, news of Sheri having been nominated for another military course, the Advance Gunnery Course at Air Defence and Guided Missile School (ADGM School, as it was called those days!) was blissful music to my years. And when someone informed me that the school was located at a place called Gopalpur-on-Sea, I couldn't help visualising myself on the sun-soaked exotic beach (a la Goa!) sipping a garnished cocktail. Given Bengaluru experience, I was confident that it would be fun.

The excitement, however, soon turned into disappointment when Sheri came back from the office and informed me that this place was nothing like Bengaluru or Goa, on the contrary it was a new institute just coming up in a remote area of Southern Orissa with poor connectivity and even poorer infrastructure. In fact, student officers could not even bring their spouses along; unlike Bengaluru, family accommodation was not available. Though disappointed, I was not the one to give up so easily. I could recall that a regimental officer of ours, Col Bunyan, had recently got posted to Gopalpur. Without telling Sheri, I established contact with him and obtained a commitment that not only could I accompany Sheri, but he would also assist us in finding and hiring suitable accommodation. With the logistics sorted at Gopalpur end, it was a breeze to get Sheri on board, Eureka!!!

Our ultimate destination (ADGM School) was situated 10 km away from Berhampur, nestled amidst the Cashew, Casuarina and the famous Ganjam Kewda (Screwpine) plantations on one side and the stunning Gopalpur-on-Sea on the other. This place offered glimpses of its past as a commercial port, with crumbling walls of ancient jetties found on the beach and ruins of several bungalows and mansions, perhaps belonging to European merchants, giving it a colonial touch.

Despite Sheri's prophetic caution and subtle indications, I had believed that all courses in the army would be like the one we did in Bengaluru, but the experience here in Orissa was different. At first, when we arrived, I quickly realised by the way the curious participants looked at me that I was the only lady who had accompanied her husband on the course. We were asked to stay outside the campus since those days the campus did not have sufficient residential accommodation, even for the permanent staff. After absorbing this initial shock, we were once again back to the familiar exercise of house hunting, though this time extended to outside the military campus in the civil area.

It was then that we stumbled upon a vast property called Padma Gardens on the way to Gopalpur beach. The property was lush green, with supposedly, a thousand coconut trees and over fifty windows. It would have been a dream country mansion, but for one major inconvenience, the property had no water connection. This meant that I had to pull water from a well. Oh my God, what! – does the Army offer this to its families? I told myself while Sheri just shrugged his shoulders as if gesturing, "I had warned you well in advance!" Notwithstanding, we moved in and despite the difficulties, we decided not to share this with our parents for fear of being summoned back home, immediately and without explanation.

The property reminded me of the grand colonial mansions in Latin America or the sprawling coconut plantations in the tropical regions of the world. I couldn't help but imagine myself as a princess in the tropics, living on a grand estate surrounded by the beauty of nature, with only the sound of coconut palms swaying in the wind as my companion – until reality struck and I had to pull out the buckets of water from the well or deal with creepy crawlies appearing at odd places and times, something which terrified me no bounds.

Sheri, too experienced his baptism into husband hood as a family man, something he realised to his chagrin, was a huge fall from the stiff stylish lifestyle he was used to so far – The '*Dandpaal sahab*' (Adjutant) in the bachelor suites of the Officers' Mess! As part of his share of household duties, he was assigned the onerous task of collecting the daily issue of entitled ration from the college on the way back from his classes. On a wet rainy day, as he was riding back from his classes on his gleaming Kawasaki Bajaj, the skies suddenly opened, and it began to pour. Unfortunately, the egg tray from the grocery bag he had placed on the petrol tank of his bike fell off, and eggs along with the cauliflower other ration scattered all over the street. It was a mortifying experience for Sheri, who always took pride in his appearance, especially in his uniform. When he arrived home, he was bursting with a lethal combination of anger and embarrassment as he announced that I would have to pack up and leave on the next flight! He couldn't stand the thought of being seen carrying groceries on his bike, and I couldn't argue with him.

But just as we began planning my return trip, we received the news that two other officers (course participants, Shamsher and Trivedi) with families would join us for the remaining duration of our stay in Orissa – perhaps another divine intervention for me! We would be sharing the bungalow at Padma Gardens with them. This was a welcome relief, as we were thrilled to have company for the rest of our stay. Our new living arrangements were quite different from the usual, isolated quarters we had been used to. We spent the rest of our time in Orissa like one big, happy family, surrounded by the lush greenery of the Padma Gardens. Our happy abode soon became a popular party and potluck venue for the rest of the course officers who often visited us. It was an experience that I will never forget. Our visitors were welcomed with fresh coconuts from the property, followed by every guest contributing to preparing eatables in my makeshift kitchen. Plates, obviously had to be the banana leaves.

In a way, our time in Orissa was like a journey back in time, with its remnants of a colonial past and its tropical, coconut-tree-lined landscapes reminiscent of the South Pacific islands. I learnt that despite the lack of modern conveniences, we could make memories that last a lifetime by creating bonds with our new family that still cling to this day. In the *fauji* way of life, it was company and togetherness that scored way over material comforts and modern amenities – a life lesson that would stand me in good stead in the days ahead.

One morning, as I was sipping my tea, I heard Sheri and Capt. Shamsher discuss a firing exercise that was going to take place on the beach. They thought it would be a terrific opportunity for their partners to go to the beach and enjoy a day out. I, being an adventurous soul, offered to take Vineeta, Capt. Shamsher's newly wedded wife, with me on my bike. On the way, we decided to pay a visit to my childhood friend, Mahima,

whose husband, Capt. Amit Rao, a coursemate of Sheri's, was a permanent staff at the College. We hadn't seen each other since our school days in Dehradun, and it was a nostalgic moment for us.

Mahima was excited to join us on the beach trip and soon enough, the three of us were off on an adventure. The challenge was that we all couldn't afford cars those days and that meant triple riding on the bike, right through the main artery of the military station. The immediate concern was that none of us could comfortably kick start the bike, the solution to which we soon figured out. To balance the bike while starting it, we found a local boy who happily agreed to help us out. We effortlessly reached the beach in no time after a thrilling, uneventful ride. We thoroughly enjoyed watching the firing exercise from a vantage point at a distance, taking in the salty sea breeze and the sound of the waves crashing against the shore and making sure that we remained out of public (read official) glare. However, on our return trip, we encountered a few hiccups along the way. As we were passing by, Sheri and Capt. Shamsher's classroom, we honked to get their attention but ended up attracting the attention of the entire class of officers, including their instructors, who were on a break, watching the scene unfold with curiosity. Our husbands were in a dilemma, not sure whether to laugh or cry at our antics. Our claim to fame arrived when the college Commandant's car crossed us - three women triple riding on a bike on the college premises and no helmets!!! By the evening, the news had spread, and we had attained celebrity (notoriety?) status, and everyone knew about our little adventure. Although we felt a bit sheepish about it, we couldn't help but laugh at ourselves and to this day often reminisce about this exciting day spent together.

Let me now paint a picture of another unforgettable adventure we experienced, a picnic on a nearby pristine beach at Sonpur! Imagine a bunch of newly married couples, brimming with excitement, embarking on a thrilling expedition to an island located across a small rivulet joining the sea. The ride to the island was uneventful, but little did we know that the real fun was about to begin! As we arrived at the rivulet, we faced the ultimate challenge — getting our motorbikes on a raft to cross over to the other side. It was like a wild, adrenaline-fuelled reality show, with all of us trying to navigate the rafts like seasoned adventurers! But once we reached the other side, oh boy, we were in for a treat! A virgin beach, untouched and beautiful, stretched before us, with no shade in sight. But did that stop us from having a blast? Not a chance! We happily frolicked in the crystal-clear waters, living our best beach life like a bunch of beach bums!

Now, here comes the icing on the cake – the most delicious meals prepared by Mahima and me. We gobbled down the scrumptious food like there was no tomorrow, and let me tell you, our appetites were as impressive as our picnic spirit! And you can't have a picnic without some groovy tunes, right? Back in those days, even the portable music players were massive, but hey, we had braved it out to carry along the biggest one out there, and we belted out songs like there was a concert on the beach!

As the sun started to set, we realised something not so pleasant – our faces had turned a lovely shade of tomato red! Ouch, sunburn alert! It turned out we had been having too much fun in the sun without any protection – we had all managed to get sunburned! For the next two days, we dealt with the pain of our skin peeling off like orange rind, but let me tell you, the memories of that wild adventure were worth it! And here's the best part – we hadn't told our friends about our little secret picnic escapade, but now, it was all out in the open! It was like a comedy of errors unfolding before our eyes, with everyone laughing at our tomato-red faces!

Oh, that was indeed one of the most momentous days of wild, carefree outings, sunburns, and laughter that still echoes through our life story as we reminisce. This little secret picnic became one of our most hilarious tales to share, and it bonded us even more than just a group of adventurous, sunburned souls!

It was soon time to leave and say goodbye to Gopalpur, Padma Gardens, coursemates, friends, and memories made with all of them together. While we were conscious that we would continue to return to Gopalpur, being the Mecca of Army Air Defence and would also continue to meet our friends as we progressed in our careers, there are some goodbyes that are forever.

Sheri was extremely attached to his beloved Kawasaki Bajaj (KB) bike, like a rider to their trusted steed. It was his trusty companion, a constant presence by his side from the days he had been commissioned. I, unfortunately, was not as comfortable on the KB and we decided to dispose of it off to a fellow officer before leaving Gopalpur. It was as if he was saying goodbye to a part of himself. It's like the iconic scene from "The Lion King" where Simba says goodbye to his father, Mufasa. The bike had been there for Sheri through thick and thin, but sometimes in life, we must let go of the things we love for the greater good. As Sheri was forced to part with his first love, I still recall the sadness in his eyes as he watched the officer come to take his bike away. The memory of Sheri and his KB will always be a testament to the deep bond that can form between a man and his ride. For me too, it remains a secret guilt I carry till date as it had been our companion across our newly begun journey from Bathinda to Bangalore and further to Gopalpur.

My sojourns in Bangalore and Gopalpur, both were experiences so distinct from each other, apart not only spatially, but also in culture and comfort. While Bangalore was a metropolitan city with all the modern-day amenities both within and outside the well-established military area, Gopalpur was in a still backward, remote area where even the military establishment was yet to evolve. State of material conveniences notwithstanding, the life lesson I learnt was profound - military life is unique and fun, regardless of the place of duty; coursemates and peer group are an extended family with whom lifelong associations and memories are created. As a *fauji* brat transiting to a *fauji* spouse, I couldn't have asked for better bedding in!

The Learning Clock – 1995

Back in Bathinda, as a newlywed closer to our hometown Patiala, I found myself becoming an essential part of my husband's family, particularly my mother-in-law, Kuki, as she was fondly referred to, within the family. My mother-in-law was a graceful, poised, sophisticated homemaker and an extremely hospitable lady who loved nothing more than a full house. Secretly, she had always dreamed of pursuing a corporate career. Despite being an incredible cook and an extremely house-proud homemaker, she nurtured a deep desire for Rohini (my sister-in-law) and me to fulfil her unfulfilled dreams of being a working professional.

Upon returning from Gopalpur, Kuki presented me with the option of pursuing further education. She asked if I wanted to do my master's degree or a B. Ed. degree. Taken by surprise and feeling a little intimidated, I chose the latter as it seemed shorter and quicker. To my surprise, even for B. Ed., I was required to take an entrance exam and secure a seat based on my score. I even tried my best not to get through. As a newly married and enjoying the best of her new role and responsibilities in her husband's battalion, why would I want to study? Yes, of course, that's what a newly married lady wants? Once married, no one tells you to study. But my mother-in-law was one strong-minded lady who was on a mission to ensure that her daughter-in-law acquired sufficient professional capability to pick up a job if it came her way.

After the exam results, accompanied by my father-in-law and mother-in-law, I went to the university for interaction and admission counselling. To my father-in-law's disappointment, my score wasn't high enough to confirm that my name was featured on the first list of admissions. He jokingly declared, "*Nakk kataa ditti teri nu ne,*" which translates to "your daughter-in-law had chopped off my nose" but implies a loss of face in society. Despite the initial setback, I now wanted to somehow secure a seat and work hard to eventually secure a graduation degree in the B. Ed. program.

As we sat there waiting for the results, Kuki's unwavering optimism was contagious. She told me not to worry and that we would try again the next day. Determined to make the most of our trip, she packed us a delicious picnic lunch the next day, and off we went. The entire day passed, and my name was still nowhere to be found on the list of successful candidates on the second day, too. I felt lost and hopeless, wandering through the halls of the university. But just as I was about to give up hope, I heard my name being announced in one of the corridors. An elderly lady approached me and asked if I was interested in studying in Ferozepur, a remote border town of Punjab. I had never heard of the place before, but Kuki chipped in and said she had spent her childhood there and was remarkably familiar with the area.

The lady then asked if Kuki was my mother, to which I replied she was my mother-in-law. The elderly lady's face lit up with joy and she expressed her admiration because I was being encouraged and backed in my pursuit of higher education by none other than my in-laws. This moment was a testament to the deep bond and love shared within our family and the lengths they would go to support each other's dreams and aspirations. I was accepted as a resident student at the Dev Samaj College of Education, Ferozepur. The place was about two to three hours of journey from Bathinda, Sheri's place of posting, and Patiala, my in-laws' residence.

As we arrived at the college campus, I couldn't help but feel a sense of apprehension at the towering walls of the hostel that seemed to resemble the notorious Tihar Prison in Delhi. It was an education college that had a central compound with a garden in the middle. While one end of the campus had classrooms, the other end had residential rooms for boarders like us. My holdall (bedding) was carried by my husband, Sheri, who by now, with great difficulty, had come to terms with my decision to pursue my further education. Yet he couldn't shake off his worries about my newfound independence and the loss of companionship.

As I was shown to my room, rather a dormitory, my heart sank as I saw I would be sharing a cramped space with seven other girls. The thought of giving up my personal space and privacy was daunting, especially with the restrooms located outside the residential premises. Sheri couldn't help but think about how much his wife, who was accustomed to a clean and comfortable personal space in her humble, yet exclusive *fauji* home, would have to adjust to this cramped and claustrophobic environment.

But despite these concerns, I was determined to make the most of this opportunity and delve into my studies with full focus. After all, in many cultures, pursuing education and personal growth is seen as a rite of passage, a way to gain independence and self-sufficiency. And so, I took a deep breath, unpacked my bags, and settled into my new surroundings, ready to embark on this exciting and enriching journey.

I was in for a surprise that evening when I set up my bedside table with a photograph of my beloved Sheri. My roommates, who were all young girls, were curious about the picture of the army man beside me and started asking questions. "Is he your brother?" "Is he posted somewhere close by?" "When will he come to visit again?" I couldn't help but smile at their innocence and excitement.

As I sipped my tea, surrounded by my new roommates, I felt a mix of emotions - excitement, nervousness, and homesickness. This unfamiliar environment was nothing like the life I was used to. I was far away from my comfortable home, my husband, and my parents-in-law. It was as if I had stepped into a completely different world.

But I had resolved to make the most of this new chapter in my life. I had pledged to my mother-in-law that I would complete my education and accomplish her unfulfilled dreams. And so, with a heavy heart, I bid goodbye to Sheri and my family, resolute in my thoughts to complete the one-year course, no matter what obstacles lay ahead.

As dinnertime approached, I could foresee myself becoming fast friends with my roommates. However, observing the extraordinary attention Sheri's photo was garnering, I soon realised that it was time to break the news to them about my marital status. I could see a hint of disappointment on their faces, but their expressions quickly changed to hope as they suggested that perhaps when their *"veerji"* (brother in Punjabi) visited next time, he would bring a group of handsome young officers with him.

From that moment on, unspoken respect and camaraderie developed in our friendship. They were happy to help with my chores and one of them even offered to use the bathroom before me, so that it would be clean to my liking. I was even told by my roommates that if I asked them to do anything in Punjabi, it would be done without hesitation. The catch was that my Punjabi knowledge was at most pedestrian. Therefore, alongside my B. Ed., it was in Ferozepur that I picked up fluent Punjabi, our native language. I wear this particular star on my shoulder with pride to this day, as I became the first sibling to speak fluent Punjabi in my family.

Throughout my time there, I was constantly reminded of the cultural contrasts between my hometown and the city I found myself in. I often thought about the different norms and customs that existed in various parts of the world, and how they shape the way people interact with each other. But despite these differences, I was grateful to have made such wonderful friends in Ferozepur. Our bond was strengthened by the common language of laughter, and I was always amused by the funny jokes that we shared. In a strange and unfamiliar place, my roommates had become my new family.

Roman Philosopher Lucius Apuleius once famously said, "Distance brings admiration;" for me, it was technically the first separation from Sheri after marriage. Weekend visits to my home and Sheri's workplace, Bathinda, therefore, became much-anticipated events which I so longingly looked forward to. It was a chance for me to escape the confines of my hostel room and spend some quality time with my husband, Sheri. However, these visits often turned out to be less than peaceful, thanks to the surprise visits from Sheri's coursemates. My culinary skills, which by now had reached some acceptability, along with my ability to entertain a group were frequently put to the test by our eleven locally posted friends, who were all excited to spend some time with the only married member of their group. I would often find myself trying to whip up a meal for this large gathering, despite my less-than-perfect cooking skills. Initially, I would sometimes land up in the kitchen to find a stack full of dishes his friends had made for me so that I wouldn't lift my finger throughout the weekend. Experience, they say, is the best teacher; I soon learned to keep these rowdies, but well-intentioned fellows under check and ensure a better weekend experience for myself. A few burnt chapatis and a bit of semi-uncooked chicken ensured that on most occasions, I was welcomed with nice, sumptuous, pre-cooked meals from the local cafeteria!

These coursemates or I would say soulmates, befriended at Bathinda, Gopalpur, and everywhere we went later during our career, however, went on to become some of my lifelong friends. Known affectionately as "the few good men" – I have precious remembrances of this extended family; to name a few - Vivek, Yogi, Navi, Gaurav, Ajay, Saby, Sidd, Goldie, Manju, Gandhi, Zubin, Jeetu, Psycho and countless more. I still smile when I think about how they used to try to convince me to stay in college and not give up, despite the challenges I faced. They were and continued to be part of my support system, always there to lift my spirits and make me laugh.

I looked forward to the upcoming weekend at Bathinda. Without fail every weekend, Sheri would have to write a formal request to the warden, explaining that I needed to visit home because of his professional duties. These visits often involved impromptu partying and merrymaking. I always appreciated the effort all my friends put into making my visits enjoyable. At times, Sheri dropped me at the station to catch my train to college on a cold winter morning on his friend's borrowed motorbike, (We found ours punctured just as we were to leave for the station) with both of us barely navigating our way through the narrow streets of Bathinda, enveloped by the heavy mist and frost on a cold January morning.

The onward journey from Ferozepur railway station to the College of Education was also worth describing. I thoroughly enjoyed it. I would take the shared *"Tonga"* (Horse carriage) and look forward to this voyage, even though it was just a short trip through the interior narrow alleys of the township.

Looking back, I can see that these visits and my time in Ferozepur, in general, were a turning point in my life. I learned to be independent, make new friends, and hone my culinary skills. It was a time that I will always revere, filled with laughter, love, and infinite remembrances. It was this expertise that was to set the motion for my roller coaster voyage ahead.

Transitioning

s the days passed, I started to feel the weight of an actual married life. Work-life balance had been a breeze so far, primarily due to the security provided by my parents being co-located. And then, one day, the inevitable happened. My parents, who had been in the close proximity so far and my go-to for everything, were transferred to Jabalpur and were to leave the month after. My husband, Sheri, had always been the strong pillar of support, but even he seemed pensive that morning. When I asked him what was wrong, he hesitated before telling me the news. I broke down in tears at the thought of my parents moving away, for I was their daughter. It was as if the umbilical cord with my parents had been snapped off. I felt I was suddenly on my own. Sheri could understand my emotions, comforted me with a warm hug, and whispered, "I promised your parents that I would always take care of you." It's a promise that he has kept to this day.

The day I got married, unlike what one is used to watching in Bollywood movies and, to some extent, in real life, I had no feelings of sorrow, of separation from my maternal home. No tears were shed, and goodbyes were with smiling faces. Many found this lack of emotion so uncharacteristically intriguing at that time, while I shrugged it off as, "Well, what's the big deal?" It was just a shifting of residence within the campus, Mom and Dad and all the comforts of the "*Maika*" were to continue. Only when this news of papa's posting to Jabalpur sunk in, nearly a year and a half after our marriage day, I could experience the departing bride's true feelings!

As they prepared to leave, my mother, Kiran, mummy, left behind a wealth of memories and possessions that she couldn't take with her. I know now that she wanted to make sure I had everything I needed to start my own home and to make sure I had the best of everything. Aren't all mothers the same? Their wealth lies in their children, and I understand after all these years.

Their departure was a bittersweet moment for me, marked by tears and laughter as we reminisced about all the good times we had shared. But it was also the beginning of a new chapter in my life as a married woman. As a young Captain's wife, the transition to military life was quite a change. The younger generation would address me as Mrs Panjrath, and the carefree routine of socialising turned into more formal interactions. Mess etiquette, table manners, social graces, and formal dressing up became second nature to us, with no formal training. This was long before the grooming institutes were even conceived, and soft skills began to be taught as subjects.

With new responsibilities came the duty of taking care of soldiers' families, as most of the troops' married quarters were in close vicinity. Interactions took place in their quarters or at large gatherings in the unit area. These meetings involved sharing experiences, addressing any problems they faced, and offering support, especially to those who had just married or left their homes for the first time. During such interactions, which my husband introduced me as my duty as an Army spouse, I began to develop a special and extremely affectionate bond with the young soldiers' wives I interacted with. While most of them belonged to South India and some of them did not understand a word of Hindi or English, I soon learnt that language was never a barrier to communicating, so long as empathy and mutual respect existed.

During one such interaction, I had a light-hearted conversation with a soldier's wife from the southernmost part of the country. I asked her how she managed her day, buying groceries, and going shopping in a town where the shopkeepers conversed in Punjabi. Her response was quick and witty – she had picked up a few keywords about bargaining and a few tricks to get the required things. Now she passed off as a local and used her expertise to help her friends. These ladies were like our brand ambassadors, taking back their experiences and learnings to their hometowns, preparing the next group of families waiting to join the forces.

On the other extreme, I had the fortune of learning from the wisdom of senior ladies, who were always around in not only guiding us in our responsibilities towards our soldiers' wives but also in tackling our personal issues and difficulties, if we had any. I could now relate to the many roles my mother performed as an army wife. I quickly picked up essential life skills and became proficient in balancing my commitments. As time passed, I became the go-to person in the unit for the most difficult tasks, and I could join in at any event at the drop of a hat. Balancing commitments became a breeze, and in no time, I looked forward to these tasks being assigned to me, as now they had turned into fun elements.

Military life taught me to be adaptable and resourceful. It was full of surprises and unexpected encounters, but I embraced them all with humour and a sense of adventure. I learnt that being strong and independent wasn't just about being physically tough, but also mentally agile and adaptable.

I cherished the nomadic life that being married to a defence officer brought with it. It gave me the opportunity to explore the length and breadth of the country, make friends from diverse backgrounds, and learn from unfamiliar cultures. And as a woman globetrotter in my own right, I will forever treasure the unique experiences and memories of my life as Mrs Panjrath.

Gopalpur's Call Again: A Seafront Sequel – 1996

While I was busy with my B.Ed. at Ferozepur, Sheri too had time to concentrate on his professional duties in the unit, as also prepare for some professional exams. The first obstacle was the Part D exam, a series of papers mandatory to be cleared for promotion to the rank of Major. Having cleared these in one go, he focused on the next major step, the Long Gunnery Staff Course (LGSC) Exam, which was a tougher, competitive exam. Only the first 24 officers in the merit list would be nominated to attend the prestigious course at the ADGM School at Gopalpur.

The timing was perfect. Perhaps, because of another cosmic intervention, my B.Ed. qualification coincided with Sheri clearing the LGSC Exam. It would be Gopalpur once again. Readers would recall that our previous trip here was quite a challenge as we had no accommodation and daily chores were difficult to navigate. However, this time around, the situation was considerably better. Initially, it was to be twelve-month tenure, extendable by another two if Sheri were to be retained as an instructor, Instructor-in-Gunnery or 'IG' being the correct terminology.

We were to be allotted housing on campus, and to our delight, we were assigned a 'Sea Facing' house, something really sought after. Though we couldn't actually see the ocean, the general direction of the entrance was in the beach's direction, some two kms away! So much for exotic terminologies and associated feel-good factor. Nevertheless, the gentle sea breeze would still find its way into our home in the evenings, providing us a refreshing escape from the heat and humidity of the day. This newfound privileged existence was not lost on others, and we quickly became the envy of our friends and colleagues. Whenever the electricity would go out (it was quite often), we would invite everyone over to bask in the sea breeze, turning an inconvenience into a fun gathering. It was a beautiful experience living in a house so close to the sea, making me fantasise I was in one of the famous seaside villas in the Mediterranean or the stunning oceanfront properties in Hawaii. It was truly a once-in-a-lifetime experience – till the power cut knocked me out of my slumber! Thereafter, kinship and camaraderie were visible at its peak.

However, life was becoming easier in Gopalpur with infrastructure development all around. We soon had a new shopping centre in the campus and fresh married accommodation. The novel Quick Shelter Scheme was also inaugurated. We had the great fortune of being the first occupants of these newly constructed quarters twice – once in the student officers' block and after Sheri's retention as an IG, in the permanent staff block. Oh, boy! What a feeling it was to move into freshly constructed government accommodation, that too with brand new specifications. Indeed, felt like royalty!

It was also during this tenure at Gopalpur that I embarked on my journey as an educator. Soon after we settled down, our university results were declared. I was over the moon to learn that not only had I topped my college, but also managed to secure a position in the entire Punjab University. Soon I was awarded a teaching appointment at the newly established kindergarten, here in Gopalpur. My family, especially my father-in-law, were proud of my achievements, with him famously now declaring, *"Kuki tere nu te kamaal kar ditta,"* meaning your daughter-in-law has done wonders. My new role as a teacher at the ADGM Pre-primary school was a genuine learning experience. I was blessed to serve under three incredible principals, Mrs Neelima Nishandar, Mrs Dogra and later, Mrs Venkatershwarlu, who helped me understand the nuances of teaching young children and consequently, grow as an educator.

But life was not just about work and serious stuff. Let me share with you a side-splitting incident during this time that still makes me giggle, though with a sharp tinge of pain in my spine. Picture this: I had just joined the school as a teacher, all excited and ready to conquer the world. And like all teachers, had used our big, majestic army school bus for my daily commute. Oh, you know, feeling like a boss!

But then, one of my dear colleagues, a senior spouse, came along on her two-wheeler, offering me the tempting option of being her pillion rider – to sit behind her and experience the thrill of scootering! It sounded fun, so the next morning, all dressed up in my finery, I eagerly awaited my two-wheeled ride.

The drive to school was smooth and delightful, but little did I know what was in store for me on the way back! As we prepared to head home, I heard my colleague murmur the quiet warning with all her politeness, something which she had done before the onward ride too "Ganiv, hold me tight, sometimes the scooter just jumps a little before getting stable."

Oh boy, I held on for dear life, thinking it would be a slight bump and we'd be on our way. But I was in for a wild traverse! The scooter channelled its inner rodeo horse and galloped like there was no tomorrow! Before I knew it, I was lying flat on my back on the road – it was like a dramatic movie scene gone wrong!

Onlookers were just as confused as I was, not knowing whether to laugh or rush to my rescue. Embarrassed to the core, my colleague and I gathered our scattered belongings and tried to get it right this time. It was a hilarious spectacle; I tell you!

Well, thankfully, our second attempt was a success, but you can bet your boots that after that wild ride, the bus became my only option for commuting! No more two-wheeler adventures for me – I was content with the cosy comfort of the big, reliable school bus!

Life in Gopalpur had its fair share of adventures and laughs, and this wild scooter ride will forever be etched in my memory as one of the most hilarious moments of that time. Lesson learned – sometimes, it's best to stick to what you know and leave the wild rides for the rodeos.

As Gopalpur continued to evolve as a station, the new starship shaped Officers' Mess was inaugurated on the imposing Kaju (Cashew) Hill, a smart, well done up building indeed. The erstwhile Officers' Mess building was converted into the Dolphin Officers' Institute (DOI) amidst big fanfare. The then Commandant, a very senior Major General, wanting to ramp up the social life, desired that the institute function every Saturday, with Tombola, dance and music. There was a hitch, though. The institute had no caterer and no movie – both being available in Berhampur city as well through cable TV at home, were big crowd dampeners, especially for the younger lot who contributed bulk of the DOI's potential clientele. This drawback prevented the DOI function from becoming a firsthand attraction. Less clientele, in turn, meant that there was not enough incentive for any contractor to provide his services – it was a vicious circle, hard to break!

But one should never underestimate the lethal combination of tact and power that comes with general ship. Not the one to give up so easily, the Commandant produced this ingenious plan. He secretly instructed the Garrison Engineer to schedule a mandatory load shedding cum electric maintenance for the officers' colony from 6:00 PM to 8:00 PM every Saturday evening. This ensured that on Saturday evenings, while the officers' colony wore a gloomy, dark look, the DOI with its powerful generator sets was bright and glowing. Soon, the crowds at the DOI started swelling up further incentivising the caterer to follow suit as he could make a quick buck while the ladies of the house got a well-deserved break, away from the kitchen as well as the idiot box – breaking the hitherto, unbreakable vicious cycle! Well, it's another story though that a few days later, a certain Col Jetley got posted to the local unit and became a regular at the DOI on Saturdays with his family. His daughter, the beautiful, Celina (later Miss India) was a natural attraction for the bachelors in town, further adding to the popularity of the DOI. Another cosmic intervention, perhaps? God indeed helps those who help themselves.

Today, DOI is a thriving club on the beach, overlooking the ocean, with a well-stocked bar and a 24x7 Cafeteria which could give any modern restaurant a run for its money. Reminiscing the difficult days of yore, one can recollect many such examples, where through ingenuity and tact, well intentioned and visionary leaders at Gopalpur have successively and incrementally ensured that this remote hamlet today vies with the best of places – there is much more to the military mind than just war fighting! Yes, this too requires innovative planning and quick decision making and beating the opposition to it.

As my journey as an educator blossomed, life took another beautiful turn on the personal front. We were going to have a baby. Excitement filled the air as my friends Ritu, Shamsher, Sumeet, Niroop, Naina, Aprajita, Gopi, Ranji, Teji, Ruth, Jitendra and later, Anu rallied around me, providing support and love during this magical but challenging time. Unfortunately, not everything went according to plan, but with my closest friends by my side, I knew I was brave and that I could get through anything. As I reflect on my journey so far, I can't help but feel grateful for all the love and support I've received, especially from my dear friends who were there for me every step of the way.

Losing a child is one of the toughest things anyone could experience. The grief is unquantifiable and the heartache immeasurable. My life took a sudden turn when my daughter was born and left us all too soon. The emptiness that came with it was beyond what words can describe.

At the time, we had completed three years and the word going around was that Sheri's tenure was expected to be extended by another two years, but my heart was yearning for a little one to hold in my arms. I shared my thoughts with the first lady, Mrs Poonam Chand, whom I hold close to my heart and who has been one of my mentors in guiding us during this challenging time. She immediately discussed the matter with her husband and before we knew it, our posting orders arrived. I felt a sense of relief knowing that we would move to a place where we could receive the proper care and support; we needed.

It's moments like these that truly show the world what a close-knit and compassionate community this fraternity is. Despite being posted in a place far from home, we had the comfort of knowing that we were surrounded by friends and family who would stand by us through the difficulties. Just like the famous quote from Winnie the Pooh, "How lucky I am to have something that makes saying goodbye so hard".

Amchi Mumbai Rhapsody
– 1999

Upon getting orders to move to his regiment in Mumbai, Sheri and I drove down from Odisha to Maharashtra, a road trip cutting through Vizag, Rajahmundry, Hyderabad, Pune and finally Mumbai. It took us three nights and four days. We arrived in Mumbai at the beautiful Kalina camp, nestled in the middle of the bustling city. We were put up in a guest room with our complete luggage in the corridor in front of our room. This two-room set would be our home till we got our accommodation; a wait which eventually lasted a long eight months!

It is in Mumbai that I experimented with a unique work environment. I started working for Citi Bank DSA Andromeda and this marked a new chapter in my professional life. The world of telemarketing was completely new to me, but the people I encountered, colleagues in the office or clients on call, were always polite and willing to communicate freely. The data I collected was managed with care and wasn't shared with multiple agencies, a refreshing change from what I was used to. Every morning, I would walk across the street to the office, feeling proud to be a part of this new venture.

I was assigned a designated space, and I worked closely with a sales executive, Rahiel, whom I recall as a lean, lanky but energetic youngster keen to learn. He was a man of few words, but I always made sure that our first impression was a good one. I made it a point to insist that he shave every morning before embarking on his client meetings. Our dynamic was a funny mix of contrasts - me, a woman, guiding the grooming habits of this man who was half my age. On the lighter side, the olive instincts popped up everywhere. The first impression was always the last one, I would brief him every morning.

I worked with Citi Bank for only a year, but it proved to be a valuable confidence boosting-experience. It was during that time, I also had the joyous news to share with everyone that I was expecting Jaskirat Singh (Kirat in short), a bundle of happiness and hope in my life after so many difficulties. Looking back, I can say that my time in Mumbai was a step forward in moving on from the hardships I had endured in the past few years and starting a new life with my family.

After conceiving Kirat, we were in a dilemma over having to travel two hours in busy traffic to Navy Nagar and deliver our baby at the INHS Ashwini the Indian Naval Hospital Ship at South Mumbai. The stories we had heard were that usually, the ladies who travelled that far often had imminent deliveries on the way itself and had to be diverted en-route to the nearest hospital. A second option was to have a standby arrangement nearer to our area of residence, which was Kalina near the Airport. We decided to get our regular checkups done at both places and have the baby in the Ankur Nursing Home, which was closest to us.

I passionately believe that God has his ways. I had surrendered myself to the Almighty's decision-making. *"Que sera sera, whatever will be will be…"* One of those days Sheri called me up from the office to let me know that his childhood friend Lily would come over to meet me. At precisely 5:00 p.m., Lily rang the bell. A pleasant-looking smart lady with a cheerful disposition smiled at me and we instantly became friends. Dr Lily Dhillon Engineer was Sheri's childhood classmate, and they had reconnected at Mumbai after a gap of almost two decades, after their junior school days. He had memories of Lily barely making it to the school bus stop, just in time, eating her breakfast on the way while her mother virtually dragged her. On the other hand, thanks to Kuki, his strict mom, Sheri was there waiting for the bus to arrive a clear 5-10 minutes in advance, all well-groomed and dressed. He was pleasantly surprised to learn that she was a doctor now, working with the prestigious Breach Candy Hospital in Mumbai, and pursuing her further studies to move abroad. She had married Cyrus Engineer, who was the Chief Administrative Officer at the Breach Candy Hospital. Both Cyrus and Lily took on the responsibility of taking care of baby Jaskirat, both before and after his arrival, and assisted us with all they could do. They were the first ones to reach out to us when baby Jaskirat was born.

The Commanding Officers' Wife was the first one to see the kiddo's heartbeat, for she would be the one taking care of me like my mother. The Commanding Officers' official car was always on standby for any requirement that might arise for me. As officers were away on deployment (it was the time our army bravely fought the Kargil Conflict) the ladies took on the responsibility for me. The initial seven months were spent being pampered by the ladies in the station. I did not have to enter my kitchen on a single day. My name had to be on the guest list, for any party happening on the campus, be it dinner or lunch. I was treated like royalty, and I never had to lift a finger to do any household chores. Upi (who was my first mentor after marriage), and Jasbir Dewan's house became my second home. Every day felt like a blessing, and I was continually enveloped by love and care. I don't think I have ever felt more loved and cared for in my entire life.

While I was carrying Kirat, Sheri was once again assigned a short course at Mhow, Indore (Madhya Pradesh) for three months, so I went along with Sheri for a month and a half. It was decided that in the last trimester, Kuki and Gurdip (Sheri's parents) would arrive with their three dogs, Tuffy, Roger, and Illat (one a Dachshund and the other two, a cross of Cocker Spaniel and Labrador). So much was their love for the pets that they hired a Qualis (Minivan) and drove from Patiala to Mumbai. We were now "house full" to welcome Jaskirat Singh. Kuki, being the nurturing soul she was, made sure that I was spoilt to the hilt, stuffing me with delicious treats and taking care of me like a queen.

But it was not only Kirat Singh's arrival that was making news in the small Kalina Camp. Our house help Roma used to take all three of our dogs for a walk on the campus; the three of them together were quite a sight. I didn't realise how much attention they drew until a newly posted officer remarked during his dine-in part, "I'm most impressed that we have one designated person who walks *all* the dogs on the campus." On hearing this, we could not contain our laughter.

It was amidst all this love and care that I entered my ninth month of pregnancy. So, there I was, in the ninth month, taking a stroll on our campus, when out of nowhere, uneasiness struck! I rushed home and shared the news with my mother-in-law, and boy, she was into action like a pro! Sheri was summoned from the office, and off we went to the nursing home, a chaotic trio on a mission!

The doctor put me under observation and booked a room for us. Well, what's the best way to pass the time in such a situation? Playing cards, of course! We played cards all day, with nothing much happening, and the doctor said, "Hey, go home and come back tomorrow at 7:00 a.m. "But guess what? The good lord above had other plans! As soon as we reached home, my pain started increasing again. It was like a perfectly timed comedy skit – just when we thought we could relax, confusion came knocking at our door again!

In the middle of the night, my mother-in-law, like a comedic alarm clock, woke up Sheri, repeating those famous words,

"It's time to go!" Sheri, half-asleep, muttered something about the doctor saying 7:00 a.m., but by then Kuki was on fire! She burst into laughter, saying, "By 7 a.m. the baby will be delivered home!"

And that's when the real chaos began! It was 6:00 a.m. when we reached the hospital, and you can imagine the madness that followed! The doctor finally showed up at 7:00 a.m., looking like he just rolled out of bed (we'll give him the benefit of the doubt), and by that time, the whole medical team had been summoned, ready for action!

Amid all this comedy of errors, Kirat made his grand entry at 10:45 a.m., in his own sweet time, like a true superstar! Oh, the pandemonium, the panic, the laughter – it was like an entertainment show fit for the big screen! Sheri's delay, my mother-in-law's frantic antics, and me in labour – a recipe for comedy gold! Was finally here! It was 13th December 2000, and he graced us with his presence for a few hours after a dramatic C-section performance. The doctors had certain concerns, and they were like, "Sheri, you better take this little Kirat to the neonatal care unit at Nanavati Hospital ASAP!"

Let me tell you, Mummy was in her A-game! She adorned little Kirat with the fanciest new clothes, making sure he looked like a true prince for his hospital debut. It was like a royal affair, with footprints being taken, and the neonatal department whisking him away – all with the precision of a grand parade. You know how Mums can be – worrywarts at their finest! Mummy had some unknown fears and was all worried about exchanging babies in hospitals. Oh, the dramatic suspense! It was like a thrilling mystery movie unfolding in the maternity ward!

After three nail-biting days (which felt like forever, mind you), he finally came back to us, unharmed. The relief was palpable, and we all let out a collective sigh of joy! He was truly a little blessing, bringing so much happiness and love to our family. Our journey was now complete, with this adorable bundle of joy lighting up our lives.

To commemorate this major milestone in our lives, we made a pit stop at the *Gurudwara* (Sikh Temple) on our way home. There, we bestowed upon him the perfect name — Jaskirat! It was like an official coronation, giving him a name that carried our love and hopes for his bright future.

The joys of parenthood and the wonders of welcoming a new life into this world – it's an emotional rollercoaster that fills your heart with so much love and happiness. And so, our little Jaskirat became the shining star of the family, making every moment an unforgettable memory in this crazy, beautiful journey of life.

I often joke that Jaskirat was our little genie, who granted all our wishes just by being born. And just like the famous "Aladdin" meme, I often say that Jaskirat is the "diamond in the rough" that we never knew we needed.

Living in Mumbai's Kalina military camp was like being shipped to a different world altogether. The campus was a hub of diverse visitors, each one more intriguing than the other. One day, a film producer turned up and expressed his interest in shooting a particular serial on the campus. Being a cinephile myself, I was naturally intrigued and couldn't help but ask what the serial (Soap Opera) was about.

To my surprise, he chose our house as the location for one episode! It had a certain semblance of a soldier's house, with boxes with names written on them. I felt like a celebrity, with bright lights and cameras set up in my home. I couldn't help but think of how different this experience was from the traditional, mundane routine of my daily life. It was like being transported to a whole different world, like something straight out of a Bollywood movie. As the shoot progressed, I could feel a sense of excitement mixed with nervousness. I was eager to see how our home would look on the big screen, but at the same time, I was wary of any potential goof-ups that might make it to the final cut.

But, as they say, "Such is life in the entertainment industry!" It was a unique and thrilling experience that I will never forget. And who knows, one day I'll even see my house on the silver screen, making a cameo in a Bollywood hit. That thought alone had me grinning from ear to ear.

While we often talk about how modern TV and social media have contributed to sensationalising news which otherwise may be trivial, I vividly recall an incident concerning an early morning newspaper report which almost turned Sheri, my husband into a celebrity (famous or notorious – depending on which side of the perception divide one was!) It so happened that there was a media briefing planned by Mumbai Sub Area Headquarters on the subject, 'Know Your Army', and Sheri's Commanding Officer was to brief the media on Indian Army's Air Defence capabilities. Being committed to something more urgent, he asked Sheri to represent him. A young Major in those days, Sheri brushed up his Air Defence knowledge and excitedly went to the conference. Being the junior most, he was the last speaker of the two-day long seminar and by the time he took to the stage, it was 2:00 p.m.

He couldn't miss noticing the conspicuously sleepy and pitiful faces of the audience. He quickly tweaked his presentation to cut out the long text and details and instead concentrated on the audiovisuals of novel Air Defence equipment in field areas or live action. Lo-and-behold, the drowsy journalists were back on alert, and he faced a barrage of questions after the brief talk.

One question caught him off guard, wherein the defence correspondent of the Times of India asked him, 'Sir, how safe is Mumbai?' Well, this being out of the scope of the seminar's theme, which was limited to basic familiarisation with the army, he tried to skip answering. However, the experienced journo was insistent and remarked, 'Sir, this is a Mumbai-specific seminar and Mumbaikars want to know how safe they are from an enemy air attack!" Left with no choice, the young officer glanced at the senior-most commander seated on the front bench, who nodded in approval – an indication that the question may be answered. So, what followed was a technical reply, "Yes, Mumbai is quite safe as there are enough Air Defence assets from all three Services i.e. the Army, Navy, and the IAF to be deployed during a contingency. In addition, Mumbai is quite far from the nearest adversary airfield. Few fighter aircraft in their inventory are even capable of reaching Mumbai on a single fuel tank because of limitations of radius of action. And even capable aircraft would be forced to fly high to conserve fuel, to avoid limiting their ability to carry a useful load of weapons, thereby risking early detection and interception by our own fighters."

Feeling satisfied with himself, Sheri returned home and retired for the day. Early morning, we were shaken out of our slumber by the shrill ringing of the phone. His Commanding Officer was on the line, anxiously enquiring, "What the hell did you do at the Seminar? Have a look at the Times of India…"

We scrambled for the newspaper and saw the bold, glaring front-page headline, "PAK CANNOT LAUNCH AN AIR ATTACK ON MUMBAI." Below the headline in small print it was elaborated, "Pakistan has limited capability to launch an air attack on Mumbai says Major XXXXXX of Indian Army's AD Regiment at Mumbai………"

Nilgiris' Cool Embrace –
Wellington Unveiled – 2002

S oon after our beloved baby Kirat's first birthday in Mumbai, we moved to a place called Wellington near Ooty, short for Ootacamund. A laid-back sleepy town in the Nilgiris (Blue Mountains) in Tamil Nadu houses the Defence Services Staff College, a prestigious tri-services institute for officers with high career aspirations. Not everybody gets a chance to go to Wellington. A proud moment for me, one of the prime points, as I had a healthy bouncing baby and a husband with a very promising career. Still… we had a long way to go. Fingers crossed!

The road trip intertwined through the thick, verdant forests, and finally, after negotiating twenty-seven hairpin bends, we arrived at our new home. Upon arrival, we stepped into a bustling reception area filled with fifty young couples like us.

So, let the fun begin! Upon reaching the Staff College reception area, we were told to wait in the oh-so-glamorous waiting lounge while the husbands dealt with the necessary paperwork. And then, guess who shows up like a grocery ninja? It was Sheri, with a bag full of groceries and some household cleaning stuff. Oh, how could I avoid comparing this grand welcome to the one we had had at Gopalpur and Padma Gardens just a few years ago? Ha ha ha!! It was *déjà vu!* But we had come a long way indeed, and the benefits of seniority and progress associated with it were more than evident.

Finally, we were guided to our allotted accommodation on the imposing Gurkha Hill. Oh, the name sounded so fierce, but in reality, it was a picturesque hilltop area housing the officers' quarters. We were allotted a second-floor apartment, nestled among other houses perched on the hill slope, with an exquisite view of the valley. You know, I could almost imagine a dramatic movie with background music playing as we approached our new home!

And to add to the special welcome, we had already been assigned a helper named Sabina. What more could a lady moving into a freshly allotted house in a new place ask for?

Now, she might not have had her kids, but let me tell you, she was a pro at babysitting. It didn't stop at that, knowing all the course calendars and events, household chores according to the schedule, and organising events – it was all second nature to her. It was like having our very own super-organised assistant! She took her role seriously, and I soon realised that she was the one in charge!

As we started setting up our home for the next year, we opened our luggage, which had been waiting patiently for us in the garage for two days. Oh, the joy of unpacking and trying to find all our essentials in a pile of stuff! It was like a treasure hunt, only the treasure was Sheri's different uniforms and my sarees!

And even before we could catch our breath, we were informed that Sheri's classes were about to begin the very next day. Talk about jumping straight into action! It was like a whirlwind of entry into a journey with mixed feelings – a warm welcome, familiar friends, friendly staff, comedy, chaos, serious business and new adventures all rolled into one.

So, there you have it, our "picture-perfect" setup at Gurkha Hills – with our enthusiastic helper, unpacking shenanigans, and classes about to start. It's like we were characters in a sitcom, and every moment was filled with unexpected twists. Army life, you never fail to keep us on our toes and deliver the most hilarious experiences! Ha ha ha!

The course routine quickly set in and there was hardly any time to think beyond the planned schedule, except perhaps on weekends. There were a lot of activities for ladies too, however, I had my hands full with my little Dennis the Menace re-incarnated as Jaskirat Singh. Let me narrate a few incidents.

One of the first planned social events of the course was the celebration of India's Independence Day on August 15th. The entire batch and the faculty gathered at the Wellington Gymkhana Club (WGC) to commemorate this important occasion. Live music was on, snacks and beverages flowing, and the ambiance was perfect for merry making. As we approached the dance floor, Sheri had this sudden realisation - my son Kirat was nowhere to be found! Sheri and I began to look for him, getting more frantic by the minute, each blaming the other for his disappearance. To our relief, we soon heard an announcement over the loudspeaker that a baby had been found trying to enter a cask of water in the pantry. We saw an officer holding him high up in the air shouting "Lost Property"! No prizes for guessing that it was little Jaskirat! We were overjoyed and relieved to have our little one back unharmed. Fancy losing your firstborn at an orderly Army premier institute, that too the Staff College!

This incident recalls the "Why you always lying'?" blame game my husband and I often played with each other.

Our son Kirat was quite an adventurous little one and, as is so typical of curious little people aged 1 to 3 years, often wandered off on his own. Since a busy road was located just outside our staircase, I was always worried that he would walk out and hurt himself. To make him toe the line, I continued the tradition of the 'Bogeyman' and warned him that an old man would come to take him away in a sack. One day, I was caught off guard when I overheard a seriously intelligent-sounding Kirat telling someone from our balcony that he knew the old man had come to take him. As I peeped outside, to my surprise, there was a frail old cobbler standing in front of our house with a sack on his back. So much for my serious threats!

Life at Staff College was yet another incarnation of the incredible course of life I had already experienced at Bangalore and Gopalpur, but on a much grander scale. It was much harder work for the husbands and even busier, socially, for the family. Imagine over three hundred officers, not only from the different regiments of the Army but also representing the Civil Service, Navy, and Air Force from different parts of the world. And since this was a competitive course, all participants were career officers, many of whom in times to come would rise to be the top Generals, Air Marshals, and Admirals in their respective services. We soon realised that we were all in the show window and had to showcase the best, in work and in pleasure; striving for excellence gradually became a habit.

While the course was primarily for officers, there were many guest lectures and events in which the ladies were encouraged to take part in. Staff College Arts and Dramatics Society (SCADS) was a popular forum where the entire family could display their talent on stage – a once-a-month event that was always a big hit. Despite my love for both music and drama, my harassed mother status (which too I enjoyed – in hindsight) prevented me from actively participating in SCADS events. However, I attended a few lectures and interactions with eminent personalities, something I consider a singular privilege that came my way. If I were to rate the best one, I would give the honours to the one by the legendary, oh-so-charming, and chivalrous, Field Marshal Sam Manekshaw.

Busy schedule and the quest for exacting professional standards notwithstanding, DSSC reinforced our belief in the adage, "All work and no play makes Jack a dull boy." In fact, the enjoyment quotient also grew exponentially at Wellington. There were loads of old acquaintances (in military lingo there are multifarious 'types' of these), many of them reconnecting after years, some for the first time after having left the academy – and then there were newly made friends, including those from overseas.

Sheri, being a 'Brig' from his NDA days, had 74 Coursemates, 26 Schoolmates, eight AD types, some Patiala types, I had some Gurkha types and of course, we had made some new friends from abroad, the *firangi* types! Imagine the state of our little house on personal occasions, be it a birthday or anniversary – there were people and children all over, from bedroom to drawing room to terrace to lobby and the snacks and liquor would run out without exception! But quick help was always at hand with neighbours quickly pitching in – after all, rainy days are part of every life!

The curriculum at the Staff College, though busy and professionally oriented, was systematically interspersed with interesting social events to break the monotony. I still vividly recall the hack rides on horseback, many treks in the forest trails of Nilgiris, weekend outings in the pretty tea gardens and wineries which were aplenty in the area, regular club evenings at WGC, and of course the fun picnics at Pykara Lake. And there were also the semi-formal syndicate get-together and course or school socials at WGC and the Five-Star Hotels in Conoor and Ooty.

For every successive Staff Course, by far the most expected outing is the South India trip. Most families in groups plan and undertake a trip through Kerala right up to the southern tip of India, Kanya Kumari. We too planned a similar trip with Gaurav, Namita, and their twins, Yuv and Yash. We all pooled in and hired a Toyota Qualis, a spacious SUV. While the couples occupied the seats in the cabin, the huge boot space, furnished with a comfy mattress, would be a playing space for the three kids. We set off from the Nilgiris on a bright sunny morning, the road meandering through the tea gardens to Mettupalayam and then to Coimbatore, the hosiery capital of India. Before we could realise it, we were on a coastal road beautifully lined with coconut trees.

The weather as well as the views were out of the world, we were supposedly in God's own country! It was indeed a wonderful outing as we touched the Guruvayur Temple with all its elephants at Thrissur, stayed on the exotic houseboats at Allepy, visited the Naval Base at Kochi, and finally got to relax and chill on the luxurious sands of Kovallam beach near Thiruvananthapuram before commencing our return journey. It was the Christmas season and as we drove through the country roads, we couldn't help noticing that every single home was decorated with a Christmas star, the religious faith of the residents notwithstanding.

Secular India at its best! En-route, we had been invited by Sheri's ex Battery Senior Junior Commissioned Officer, who had recently retired, to stay with him at Thrissur. Sheri's unit consisting of troops from the four states of Southern India, there was a sizeable presence of Keralites. Since Gaurav consented, we accepted the invitation to stay the night at Subedar Vincent's house. Expecting a homely welcome, we were in for a pleasant surprise when we reached his village. Not only had the family taken great pains to make us comfortable in a beautiful mansion arranged by Vincent sahab through his friend, but he had also invited all ex-servicemen and their families belonging to nearby places who had served with Sheri for a grand Christmas feast. And boy, did they oblige – they were all decked up and ready to receive and host their dear *saahab,* in their re-attired home.

It was the most touching and amazing experience we could ever dream of, to end our holiday - reliving the unit days where Christmas is celebrated with great fervour and joy as a regimental festival. It reinforced our belief that the regiment is indeed one enormous family and associations developed with our soldiers and their families last forever! Of course, it was also a memory that Gaurav, Namita, and the three children cherish to this day; making memories and bonds to last a lifetime!

We spent a wonderful year in the salubrious climate of the Nilgiris, residing on a hilltop. Time passed quickly and before we knew it, it was time to move on to our next adventure. The MS branch (HR people of the Army) had been working on the postings post-completion of the course and speculation was ripe in the air. On the day of reckoning, after an anxious wait, our transfer orders were dropped into our official post boxes (known as lockers in Staff College lingo). As expected, Sheri was shortlisted to proceed to a non-family station.

For Kirat and me, it meant a two-year long separation, though it was good for Sheri as far as career experience was concerned. While others were rejoicing over their impending move, I was extremely worried, and the next few days were spent in careful planning. What would be our selected place of residence? Would we be permitted to visit Sheri occasionally? How much leave would he be able to get? How would I manage as a single mother for these two years? So many questions flashed across my young mind, adding to the anxiety. I could not help but relate to what Mummy would have gone through in similar circumstances when we were kids. That's when

enlightenment struck - *if she could, so would I.*

Our sojourn at Wellington was memorable and a reminder of the importance of family, friends, and the joys of parenthood. We

had indeed grown as individuals and had also substantially enhanced our circle of acquaintances. The fast-paced nature of time was reminiscent of the concept of "Carpe diem" in

Latin culture, where one is encouraged to seize the day and make the most of every moment.

In Anxious Hours, The
Comfort of Patiala– 2003

Sheri was reassigned to a new station that was not within proximity to any of the military stations designated to house the Field Area Family Accommodation, colloquially called 'Separated Family' or SF accommodation. At the time, I was informed by my friends that the area was a 'hot' one, not in terms of climate, but rather in terms of the level of activity and importance of the assignment. Little did I know what that truly meant. This was the first time that Sheri and I had to be separated, and it was to last at least two long years. I recall feeling like my soldier husband was being deployed to a foreign land, leaving his loved ones behind.

On hind sight, it was reliving my mother's journey when my father would be posted to non-family stations. Life had indeed come full circle. The news was shared with both sets of parents and families. Thus began the planning of parking me with our little belongings at Patiala, Sheri's hometown.

In psychology, this experience is known as the concept of "Separation Anxiety", where spouses are separated from their loved ones for an extended period, causing them great distress. However, I tried to find comfort in humour and found solace in memes such as "When you miss bae but you gotta adult (You are forced to behave like an adult)." It perfectly captured the feeling of missing someone dearly, but still having to carry on with daily responsibilities.

Despite the difficulty and distress of separation, I remained positive and looked forward to the day when we would be reunited. Our love and commitment to each other only grew stronger with every passing day. I reinforced thoughts that my mother too had been in similar situations being an officer's wife herself, and I mustered up all my courage from her example.

That's when we finally moved to Sheri's hometown in Patiala, Punjab. His parent's home was currently unoccupied as papa was on a post-retirement assignment at Hubli. Initially, it proved to be a challenging time, when Sheri had to leave us and proceed to his place of duty. I was young and regretful of not exploring the option of non-family accommodation at the time, as it would have allowed Kirat to join a better school with more children of his age group, with me having friends among other ladies who were in the same situation. Notwithstanding, we soon adjusted and began exploring ways to get on with circumstances in the best possible manner.

To keep myself occupied, I took up a job as a teacher at the very school in which Kirat was enrolled. Meanwhile, Kuki and papa relocated to Hubballi (Hubli), lock, stock, and barrel. Although Sheri promised to keep in touch, it was tough being separated from him as there was no mobile phone service where he was located. I found comfort in small doses of updates from him and was overjoyed when we were granted permission to visit him twice during his assignment. These visits took us to some of the most remote areas in the furthermost underdeveloped part of Jammu and Kashmir.

To lighten the mood, I often joked with friends about how I was 'living like a single parent' and shared jokes about the challenges of raising a child on my own. Despite the difficulties, I remained strong and focused on the future, when we would finally be reunited as a family.

As the days passed, I learned and imbibed a lot during the time I spent in Patiala. The slow pace of life and the warm and welcoming community made it feel like home in no time. I quickly made friends with the regular inhabitants, and everyone knew me in just a few months of our stay there. The small-town charm was unmatched, with shopkeepers recognising my husband from his childhood, and reveling in the fact that now they knew our son too. The neighbours were always ready to offer precious advice and support whenever I needed it. Soon it felt as though I had been living in Patiala for ages.

The tight-knit community in small towns like Patiala is something that I had never experienced before. It is in stark contrast to the fast-paced life in big cities, where people are often too busy to take the time to get to know each other. In Patiala, every day was filled with laughter and good company, and it was a place where I truly learned to thrive as a woman.

Life in general was comfortable, laid back, and I was surrounded by a community that had become like family to me. I had made countless friends and was known to everyone in the small town. But despite the peace and tranquillity of our daily lives, there were occurrences and incidents which made us long to be together as a family.

On an otherwise fine weekend, my son, Kirat, suddenly fell ill, things took a sudden turn when Kirat's prolonged cough and cold was diagnosed with pneumonia. It was a scary time for me as a mother and I felt completely helpless as Sheri wasn't around to help me deal with this situation – something I had never handled alone so far. While there is a full-fledged Military Hospital (MH) at Patiala, staying in a civil colony and with no immediate military neighbours, I was not noticeably confident about approaching the MH directly for help. As I sat by Kirat's bedside in the hospital, praying for his health and well-being a week later, the outpouring of love and support from our neighbours was heartwarming. They rallied around us and offered their assistance in every way possible, from taking care of Kirat to providing moral support for me. It was a priceless indication of the intense sense of community and camaraderie that exists in small towns. Even Sheri's course-mates and fellow officers posted at Patiala were a tremendous help and seemed to have emerged from thin air to assist me and Kirat. The fighter in me had woken up and the battle against the dreaded fever started. With a few IVs infused with antibiotics, it came down gradually with time.

Very soon, Kirat made a complete recovery, and I was grateful for the support and care that our neighbours and friends had shown us during this tough time. It was an experience that I will never forget and one that I will always cherish.

Another incident from my time in Patiala still sends shivers down my spine, and it's a tale that blends suspense and a touch of humour. Our standalone house was practically a fortress, thanks to the multitude of SOPs (standard operating procedures) enforced by my mother-in-law. These included a nightly routine of checking doors, windows, and latches, and finally depositing the garbage in the bin near the gate.

One windy evening, as I was diligently finishing up my chores, I heard a deafening bang. To my utter horror, the main door slammed shut, leaving my mischievous 3-year-old, Kirat inside our rather sizable house. Panic gripped me. What if the lights went out? What if he began to wail in fear? What if he got himself into some toddler predicament?

We tend to secure our homes like impenetrable fortresses, but this time, I was the one locked out, and it was mentally exhausting. I had to think on my feet. I began to call out to Kirat, telling him that I was trapped outside, and he had to come to my rescue. The little one understood his mummy was in distress, and he was the hero needed for a daring rescue mission.

I instructed him to drag a chair over to the door and work his magic on the latch. He happily obliged, lugging the chair with the determination of a pint-sized superhero. Next in line was the wire mesh door, and, to my amazement, he skilfully managed to open it. It was a true comedy of errors turned suspenseful situation, and I heaved a sigh of relief as I was finally back inside with my little hero.

Once, my mother-in-law was visiting me in Patiala, and we both decided to have a movie day. We headed to the theatre and had a blast watching the film. But here's where the comedy starts – on our way back, we hopped onto a cycle rickshaw, and guess what? The rickshaw puller took us directly to our doorstep, like a pro GPS navigator!

My Punjabi-speaking mother-in-law, with all her curiosity, asked the rickshaw puller how on earth he knew the way. And boy, did he have the best response ever! With a grin on his face, he said, "Who doesn't know Bibiji? She's the noble teacher whom I've had the honour of chauffeuring many times, along with her little Kirat!"

We couldn't stop laughing! This simple rickshaw puller recognised me as a soldier's spouse and even remembered the times he'd taken us on his rickshaw joyrides. I mean, talk about fame, right? It was like being in some comedy movie, where the rickshaw puller becomes our unofficial chauffeur, aware of our whereabouts and giving us VIP treatment! We were laughing so hard that we almost fell off the rickshaw (well, not really, but you get the idea).

In that hilarious moment, we knew we must have left quite an impression on this rickshaw hero. And you know what? It's these little unexpected connections that make life so much fun! Who knew that a simple rickshaw ride would lead to such a comical encounter?

My stay in Patiala alone with Kirat made me realise I had often taken for granted the significant resources in the form of security and support that I had received, thanks to my spouse's service in the armed forces. However, it also strengthened me and made me more resilient. I became a person capable of handling any eventuality on my own.

The olive blood running through my veins gradually changed from red over those formative years. I wasn't taught to be a patriot, to shout a war cry, or simply to smile when passing an Army convoy on the road. The transformation occurred with no prior notice.

The realisation dawned upon me that the once shy and reserved person had evolved into a confident decision-maker who could handle life's challenges independently. My Patiala stay concluded with this profound awareness.

Juggling Jalandhar – 2005

Before we realised Sheri's tenure in the field came to an end, it was time to fall back to the regiment, which was also moving to Jalandhar. In the process of settling into Jalandhar, as we bid adieu to the memories of Patiala, I found solace in the profound bonds of family. Whether amidst the simplicity of a small Patiala town or the dynamic bustle of Delhi, the warmth and encouragement from loved ones and peers give a place its sense of belonging. This universal truth resonates across cultures and boundaries, a sentiment shared by all. The excitement of setting up home after two years of staying apart knew no boundaries. We packed our belongings and drove down to our new place of work.

Jalandhar presented a nurturing environment for Kirat's education. We admitted him to the best school, most instantly as Kirat liked the yellow bus that came to pick kindergarten children from home. There was no further discussion, it had to be the yellow bus and green uniform. His education began almost immediately upon our arrival at the new station. I too aspired to pick up a job as an educator. One of the premium institutions offered me a fulfilling teaching position. Soon, I cultivated a new circle of friends with whom I began carpooling. The mundane turned into delight, and time seemed to slip through our fingers effortlessly.

Sheri, in his exuberance, changed his four-wheeler and indulged in a better upgrade. One evening, the regiment planned to go for a social event together. We safely parked it in the Officers' Mess and off we went to enjoy the evening. Upon our return, we saw the staff in a frenzy and shaking. Sheri, to his horror, found his two-day-old four-wheeler purchase had been mowed back by a 2.5 Tonner heavy truck carrying troops' food. Apparently, on reversing, he could not fathom the distance correctly. Anyway, troops are our family, and everyone makes mistakes. The insurance company took care of the damage and the boys learnt from their oversights. It is the leader who must be humble in his actions and guide his men through tough times.

Very soon, we were among the first few officers to be allotted accommodation out of turn, as Sheri was coming in from a non-family station. The new home was inviting and we were looking forward to settling down as a family, now that the admission process, new job for me, and the new car were in place. We opened our belongings, decorated our home, and settled in. Life was looking brighter than ever. Family time and friends to socialise with, were in abundance.

Jalandhar had an interesting background being one of the oldest cities in northern India. Similarly, the Jalandhar Cantonment area is also known for its ancient antiquity in India. This cantonment was established by the British after the first Anglo-Sikh War of 1848. My maternal grandfather had been posted here during his service days. My mother used to attend the school where I eventually taught. The news of getting posted to this place brought sparkles in her eyes and she decided to come and relive her younger days. The small market called *sadarbazaar* was our first stopover. We began the fun by gorging on the famous lentil fritters known as the "*Jawali Ke Pakore*". She exclaimed they hadn't changed in texture or taste in the last fifty years. Who would fail to acknowledge the famous sweetshop? Lovely Sweets. The quaint sweetshop serves the most delicious sweets all over the country. So much for a town that has an abundance of industrial infrastructure. It is the oldest cantonment which had witnessed almost one century of British rule. It features grand British-era bungalows, in one of which my grandparents had resided almost five decades ago. No sooner had we settled in and our respective families had savoured the memories and flavours of their time spent here, we were informed about Sheri's unexpected move on another posting to Delhi.

While Sheri moved to Delhi, we shifted to the Officers' Mess accommodation which had a spacious room and an attached kitchen. Kirat and I stayed back to complete our academic year. His fourth birthday was celebrated on the premises of the Mess and that's where he learned to be a master of his two-wheeled bike. The staff of the Officers' Mess became our guardians and supported us in all ways. For life in the battalion becomes your primary home. The people who are posted with you become your family and create the most unique bonds. Well, that's the irony of life. Little did we fathom; that the story was far from over. As soon as he joined the new assignment in Delhi, he was informed about another twist in the tail- this time it was a selection to attend the Staff

College course abroad. Usually, such assignments were nonfamily, but in our case, it was pleasantly different. He got an assignment to do a year-long course in Bangladesh, an opportunity we enthusiastically embraced.

We had precisely forty-eight hours to move after his clearance. When we broke the news to our parents, both mothers were taken aback. Happiness galore, they prayed for our safe travels and a professionally enriching tenure.

Reflecting, on our time in Jalandhar, which spanned only six fleeting months. Prior relocations had always been lengthy affairs—first, the Officers' Accommodation was a challenge. Initially the interim dwellings, thereafter, culminated in a permanent residence. However, this unique tenure had seen us move directly into a permanent abode before eventually temporarily returning to the Officers' Mess.

This journey of ours underscores a vital life lesson: expectations do not always align with reality. Surprises, both pleasant and challenging, pepper our path, demanding that we stride forward with resilience. Though the road might not always unfold as envisioned, it's these unexpected turns that add colour to our narrative. Embracing these surprises and looking ahead to the next chapter, we gather experiences that shape our lives in ways we could never predict.

As I recall, it was a typical day in Patiala. Kirat and I were going about our daily routine when suddenly my phone rang. It was my Nani, whom I hadn't heard from in a while. She had a desperate tone in her voice, and I could tell that she was calling with an important message. She told me she was missing me terribly, and that I had to come to Delhi as soon as possible.

D-328, A Haven of Familial Love and Togetherness— 2005-2010

Travelling back to the phone call from my maternal grandmother in Delhi, I was taken aback by my grandmother's request to visit her immediately. My Nani had never been one to demand visits, and I couldn't understand why she was so insistent on me coming over. I knew my parents had recently moved to Delhi to take care of my grandparents, and I was a little concerned that something might be amiss. We booked our tickets and proceeded. Upon arriving, I was greeted by my complete maternal family. My parents and Nani were there, as were my two aunts, Arshi and Simran.

As we walked into my grandparents' house, the familiar warm, and comforting atmosphere enveloped me. Mummy was already waiting for us outside the house, eagerly expecting our arrival. I hugged her tightly and could feel her relief wash over me in that embrace. But as we settled down and unpacked, she brought up the possibility of her being diagnosed with cancer. I was in shock, unable to believe what I was hearing. It just didn't seem fair that someone as kind, brave, and selfless as my mummy would have to endure such a challenge.

Let me give you a brief background. As Mahip papa approached his retirement, his last station was Banbasa, a small remote station on the borders of Nepal. Retirement was around the corner and Gini was undergoing issues on her marital front. She had to recollect herself and Jas (her son) was with them. The maternal grandparents invited them to stay with them at Delhi as they too were entering their twilight years, yet independently. Their First floor was vacant and in return, mummy had to take on the complete responsibility of the eldest daughter in the family.

As for papa, he wasn't content with the thought of just sitting around and enjoying his golden years. He was a person of action and wanted to continue making a difference. So, on superannuation, he took up various positions with different organisations, including Aero Star Aviation, where he was tasked with procuring Sikorsky Helicopters from the United States and was handpicked to be trained at their plant at Stratford, Connecticut. Papa even went on a deputation to Nepal as the Country Head with the Checkmate Securitas group, showcasing his unwavering spirit and adventurous nature.

However, despite a promising post-retirement career opportunity for my father in the corporate world, my mother set base in Delhi to look after my ageing grandparents, who were now beyond 80 years. So, while papa continued to dabble in corporate jobs befitting his status and capabilities in and around Delhi, Mummy assumed control of D- 328 Defence Colony as a full-time family manager and caretaker and got busy keeping the family together. She was the backbone of the family, running the kitchen, hosting friends and family, and ensuring everyone was well-fed and happy. She was like a superhero, juggling multiple roles and still finding time to smile and spread joy. For she thought of the times her parents had taken care of us when she had to stay back many times while papa was away on his many remote area assignments.

As I sat back and thought about the lives my parents were leading, I couldn't help but think of the famous adage "Retirement: When you switch bosses from the one at work to the one at home." But in my parents' case, they were bossing it up both at work and at home, making everyone bond into stronger ties and filling us with gratitude for our family's unwavering love and support.

Nani's house in Delhi was always abuzz with laughter and happiness. It was in the city's heart, making it convenient for all her grandchildren to visit. As the eldest daughter, my mother played a significant role in ensuring Nani's well-being and happiness. Whenever the family gathered at Nani's, it was a time for celebration. *Nani* would insist on preparing a mouthwatering spread of tea and snacks carefully curated from the local Defence Bakery, along with Samosas and Gulab Jamuns from Anil Sweets, also in the Defence Colony market.

The gatherings at Nani's were a time for everyone to catch up, share their stories, and simply bask in the warmth of each other's company. For Nani, seeing her children and grandchildren laughing and sharing their lives was a source of joy and sustenance that would last for weeks to come.

These gatherings were an accurate representation of the saying "The family that eats together, stays together." And Nani's house was the glue that kept us all together, providing us with a warm and cosy home away from home. To put it simply, Nani's house was the hub of laughter and love, and the memories created there will forever hold a special place in our hearts. Growing up, I was always fascinated by my Nani and Nana's simple yet disciplined way of life.

I remember my Nani, affectionately known as "Deep" by my grandfather, as a warrior too who battled cancer not just once, but twice in her lifetime. Despite the odds, she was a fighter who persevered and triumphed over the disease, living a full life until the ripe old age of 88. Her story of resilience and strength was so remarkable, it even found its way into the annals of medical history at AIIMS, where her case was studied and spoken about among the medical fraternity.

She had the most amazing closet. I remember as children we enjoyed opening her Almirah. Her clothes were stacked neatly, and patiently she would take out her set of clothes to wear, and stack clothes from the previous day, washed and ironed by herself in the designated place. She had these beautiful satin *Nadas* (drawstrings) from the time of her wedding; and every day, she would handpick her attire with precision.

Her home had only essentials. Neat, clean, with enough room for every necessity, without unnecessary frills. And yes, everything had to be in its place where it could be located easily. Their home reflected their systematic, organised, and tidy way of life with the right balance of warmth and coziness, which attracted family members of all generations. Everything listened to them, the fans knew the speed they liked, and the television would also obey my grandfather.

She lived life to the fullest, never letting her illness impede her zest for life. Her indomitable spirit was an inspiration to us all, reminding us that it's never too late to overcome challenges and live life to the fullest. She was a testament to the proverb, "where there's a will, there's a way."

Nani was truly one in a million, and her legacy lives on through the memories we hold dear of her and the lessons she taught us about courage, strength, and the power of the human spirit.

My Nana, a retired colonel from the Army Service Corps, had a specific way of doing things, and everything in their home had to be just so. After my Nana had a cardiac arrest in his late forties, discipline in their lifestyle had assumed utmost importance. They followed a strict routine: waking up at 5 a.m., Nani preparing tea and Nana picking up the newspaper. Nana would then go to the Gurudwara and come back to a breakfast prepared by Nani, followed by discussions on family and current affairs.

Nani and Nana would sit in the garden and enjoy fruit-based snack at 11 a.m., followed by lunch at 1 p.m. sharp and siesta thereafter. Tea was served at 4 p.m., and thereafter would go for a long walk. Upon coming back, Nana would sometimes have a drink with my papa, and dinner was laid at 8 p.m. The news was on the television and lights were out by 9 p.m., and the entire family respected and adhered to their routine.

This simple and orderly way of life is a rarity in today's fast-paced world, where chaos and confusion stemming from having to run faster and faster on the treadmill of daily life is the order of the day. But Nani and Nana's disciplined routine was a lesson in the beauty of a calm and structured lifestyle, reminding me of the traditional Japanese concept of *"wabi-sabi"* which values simplicity, imperfection, and the acceptance of transience. For the concept of minimalism was coined by them long before it was conceived.

Over the next two days, mummy underwent a battery of tests to confirm the prognosis. It was a difficult and uncertain time, but my mother's bravery and unwavering determination never wavered. She was a true inspiration.

Kiran was a true fighter. Despite receiving the devastating news of her Stage III breast cancer diagnosis, and that it had already spread to her lymph nodes, took on the challenge of chemotherapy and radiotherapy head-on. With her positivity and determination, she went into remission for five glorious years.

I realise now that it was destiny that brought them to Delhi. It was here the two strong resilient ladies became a support for each other. Nani was constantly supporting Kiran during her surgery and postoperative treatment. The silent fighter in them which had seen them support their respective families while their spouses were away on military duties, always remained alive and saw them through the current crisis.

It was during this time, that my papa fulfilled Kiran's long-standing desire to visit her daughter, Gini, and her children in Melbourne, Australia. Mummy was now blessed with two grandsons, Jaskaran and Jaskabeer, whom she was eager to meet and bond with. The trip was an emotional and energising experience for her, filled with happy memories that she treasured for the rest of her life.

When I look back, it was her sheer will to survive only due to positive familial bonds. These were the connections we grew up with. More about Kiran later.

Dhaka - Bangladesh Jabo?? – 2006

We landed in Dhaka as the sun was making its way down the horizon. Navigating through the city's chaotic streets felt like an extreme sport, a mix of dodging rickshaws and deciphering the honking symphony of horns. Dhaka, with its bustling energy, was like an espresso shot straight to our cultural senses.

Our home for the stay was the SAARC Block, a real-life version of a diplomatic chessboard. Imagine, the Indian Airforce officer's morning view was a direct stare-down with the Pakistan Airforce counterpart! It's like they were playing "who blinks first?" every day. Meanwhile, the Indian Army shared casual glances with the Pakistan Army, not quite a staring contest, but a friendly game of "I see you."

On the third floor, the Navy folks were just chilling, probably swapping sea stories and discussing the best maritime routes for cargo ships. The actual surprise was discovering that even amidst all these official tensions, our cultures were practically secret twins. The food was a delicious déjà vu; the dances felt like a homecoming jig, and the singing sessions were like a choir of nostalgia. It was as if Dhaka was trying to remind us of, we're all in this world together.

After the first week of getting lost, finding our way, and narrowly escaping rickshaw collisions, the college welcomed us with open arms. The classes hit us like a monsoon downpour – intense and overwhelming. But amidst the academic whirlwind, there was one standout moment: Kirat, our little Sikh wonder, stepping into a local school. However, his *patka,* the small turban he wore, confused his classmates. So, I bravely ventured into the world of education diplomacy and gave the Principal a crash course on Sikhism and the art of turban-tying. The result? The entire school became turbantastic, and they even added 'turban tying' to their extracurricular list.

Kirat became the unofficial cultural ambassador, forging friendships faster than a cheetah on caffeine. It was like a mini–United Nations summit in the playground – sharing traditions, trading stories, and debating whose national dish was the most delicious.

The culture and residents of the country embraced with utmost warm-heartedness. It was interesting to see everyone wanting to invite us over, showcase their hospitality. An interesting time was the holy time of fasting. A spate of invites flooded us for Iftar, making us aware of the most humbling experiences. The families prepared a vast array of exotic dishes and offered them with the utmost love. We realised that the country of Bangladesh was full of warmth and affection.

Speaking of diplomacy, one day our neighbour was all set to travel to Pakistan during a break. Kirat, in his innocent curiosity, asked where she was headed. She replied, "Pakistan, of course!" Kirat, with the candour only a child can muster, dropped a truth bomb. "I'd love to tag along, but my folks think Pakistan is our arch-nemesis." Cue my embarrassing scream, followed by our neighbour's chuckles and a diplomatic "Don't worry, it's true."

In the heart of Dhaka's market, Baridhara, where we used to go for our grocery shopping every week. A scene worthy of a heartwarming scene caught my attention: a Bengali-speaking Sikh family. I was more surprised than if a unicorn had strolled by doing the cha-cha. I had to know their story, and soon, we were bonding over textiles and trading numbers. Turns out, they were garment industry quality control aficionados – I mean, who knew garments and turbans could blend so seamlessly? Next few months were endless meetings, travels picnics, and layovers at their place. Fridays were preserved to visit the gurdwara near the famous Dhak Eshwari Temple. We were always hosted with so much hospitality. In no time, their son and Kirat became inseparable.

It was time for our country's presentations to take place in the military college. Sheri prepared his opening speech with the melodious Manoj Kumar hit movie number *"Hai Preet Jahaan Ki Reet Sadaa"* PURAB AUR PASCHIM, 1970. The land where love is a tradition and we bring before you the warmth from India, where we belong. True to its words, the presentation highlighted people in true equivalence, and we took part as a family. Holding our heads high and taking pride in showcasing the country we symbolised on a foreign land. The delightful evening ended with delectables from India.

Speaking of ladies' interaction, it came with vibrant colours and ladies coming together from 33 countries. Amalgamation of rich cultures, blending performances by attending participants. Hosting the International ladies was so enriching as all counterparts wanted to display their best. It was an evening to recall. We were efficiently equipped by our experiences in India.

Our days turned into weeks, and as our time in Dhaka ended, I was hit by a cocktail of emotions. The excitement of the next adventure mixed with the sadness of bidding farewell to my newfound friends made me feel full of mixed emotions.

But just as our Bangladeshi chapter was wrapping up, life served up a plot twist: a call from Kuki, my mother-in-law and confidante, dropped a bombshell. Cancer was knocking, trying to crush her party. With Kirat in tow, I rushed back to Patiala to be her unwavering support. The surgery lights flickered, and the chemotherapy began.

Despite the cancer cloud, Kuki's spirit shone brighter than a supernova. She was a cancer-battling wizard. Meanwhile, Kirat became a professional "mom-sharer" – friends would rotate, braiding his hair, managing exams, and trying to fill my absence with parental wisdom like, "Yes, ice cream counts as dinner."

Even with her past struggles with cancer twenty-three years ago, Kuki remained strong and optimistic throughout her battle with cancer. She was a true inspiration to all who knew her. And through it all, the military community, like a platoon of superheroes, swooped in. Just like they rallied around my sister and me during my mom's illness back in Dinjan, they had our backs yet again. In between hospital visits, chemotherapy rounds, and Kirat's expertly braided hair by the ladies of the regiment in my absentia, life continued its dance. Over the next seven years along with her treatment, Kuki saw many milestones – weddings, grandkids, and everything in between. She was blessed with quality time to travel, to spend time with us, even to visit Rohini (Sheri's younger sister), and more – a real-life victory lap.

As we said goodbye to Bangladesh and embraced the next journey — a posting to New Delhi our memories stayed painted in vibrant cultural hues and bound by unbreakable ties. Dhaka had taught us that amidst the chaos, connections and camaraderie make life's tapestry truly exceptional.

Delhi Calling Again –
Pavilion Chronicles, 2007

After an infinite juggling with plans, we zeroed in to move in directly into hostel accommodation. We unloaded the truck there. We had had enough of nomadic adventures in our previous tenures. A small dwelling with every bit of essentials.

Unfortunately for Kuki, the diagnosis was complicated, and to continue her treatment, we had to bring her to stay with us in Delhi. It was not a fortunate situation for her as she was a house-proud lady and wanted to continue her stay in Patiala. I, on the other hand, wanted to gather myself and be in a larger space for her medical emergencies and keep Kirat's requirements of being closer to his father.

As we settled down in our environs. I was pleasantly surprised to find Marlene as my next-door neighbour. A woman with a captivating demeanour, mesmerising grey eyes, eloquent English, and a fantastic dressing sense. A friend you would love to emulate for her fantastic talent in remembering dates and sealing friendship goals. She introduced me to an interesting job opportunity as a guest coordinator at a mall called Lotus and the company was Cottage Industries Exposition; exporter of silk carpets.

We were a group of ten ladies who had to work for only four hours in the morning. A sari for uniform and a nameplate to distinguish ourselves. We turned heads when we walked on the roads of our campus. It was a life-changing experience for me. As Armed forces spouses, we have an aura around us, and this organisation teaches us to be confident in all situations. After this interview, it was a cakewalk for me.

Kuki mummy on the other hand, would support me in dropping and picking us up from work. Kuki would enjoy her short trips as they would help her forget the challenging times she was going through. It would also save us from the many hitchhikes we had done with officers going to work from home to Sena Bhawan amidst the traffic jams in front of the Subroto Park crossing. Saving time to reach work on time. Shhhh! the cats out of our bags. Marlene and my association grew with time and lasts till date.

Kiran mummy had her series of checkups going on. She was in remission. The Research & Referral hospital became our space for meet ups between mothers. The cafeteria would serve me *"Chola Bahturas."*. Indian delicacy comprising chickpea gravy with puffed deep fried puris and coffee. It was here that I witnessed at such close length various stages, types and age groups undergoing a complicated series of treatment. The medical fraternity which deals with the emotional outburst and is sensitive to its patients. For the journey is tough, long, and the outcome is unpredictable. The only hope is by being positive. Caregivers like us need counselling and healing. Our strength lies with the vigorous support and backing of such a strong organisational support behind us.

The Spanish Proposal - Hola! – 2007

It was during these trying times that Rohini announced her association with Miguel, a Spanish national from Madrid. Unsure of what to expect in the future, my sister-in-law invited the complete family to our hometown in Patiala Punjab.

I recall the time they got married. When Miguel had popped the question, Rohini had a unique request for him. She told him that he would have to personally ask for her hand in marriage from her parents. And so, Miguel and his entire family, including his mother Teo, Father Mariano, and brother Jharvey, made the trip from Spain to India.

They were staying with us in Patiala, and one morning after a busy day filled with sightseeing and travel, we were all sound asleep. Miguel and Teo woke up early and quietly set about making breakfast for everyone. They prepared the most delicious Spanish omelettes and other specialties that they had brought from Spain. Kuki, who was usually the one in charge of the kitchen, was astounded at the sight of our guests taking over. But it was truly a delight to see the spread on the breakfast table and to taste the delectable treats that they had made for us.

It was an unexpected and heartwarming gesture, and it just goes to show how cultures can come together and find common ground in the simplest of things, like cooking a meal together. Here it's important to bring in the humorous aspect that was heretofore unheard of, the prospective groom's family fixing meals and cleaning the utensils at the bride's house. It was unusual of, and my mother-in-law was astonished. It was truly a memorable moment that made us humbled and appreciate the traditions that span across the world. Miguel and his family had won us over with their warmth.

There was another moment of pure comedy as my father-in-law and Mariano, set off for a couple of drinks at the club. The language barrier was quite a hurdle, as Mariano could only speak Spanish and my father-in-law only spoke English. But that didn't stop them from enjoying each other's company. Kuki, always the problem-solver, put our address in Mariano's pocket to cater for an eventuality, should he get lost.

The sight of these two, who had just met each other, off on a mission to find the nearest club for a couple of beers was something I'll never forget. The expression on Kuki's face was a mix of amusement and disbelief. I could tell she was wondering what was going to happen next.

What happened at the club remains a mystery to this day, but both men returned on a cycle rickshaw with big grins on their faces, looking happy and content. It was a humorous prompt that despite language barriers, a love for good drinks and a respectable company can bring people together in unexpected ways.

It was decided that the venue would be Delhi and that the Groom's family would come down from Spain. The dates were sealed. Sheri and mummy took on their charter of duties. It was a reminder of our wedding. The only difference was that things were more streamlined, as decor and food were outsourced, and we could enjoy the event too.

It was four days of fun and frolic, coupled with wedding rituals. At the back of our minds, Sheri's move was expected any day. It made us realise that time and tide wait for no one. What must happen eventually happens. Fulfilling his responsibility as an elder brother and a responsible son, he looked forward to delivering his soldierly duties.

Rediscovering Eastern Elegance – The Year 2008

As Sheri climbed the ranks to become a Colonel, life for me took a wild turn as I transformed into the proverbial Commanding Officers Wife(COW). With the new title came a flood of responsibilities, challenges, and a surprising number of comical moments, grooming sessions, and instances where I wore the hats of both a mother and an elder sister.

Our grand plans to return to our parent unit after Sheri's promotion were dashed when destiny decided to throw us a curveball. Instead of commanding in style, Sheri was assigned to raise a new unit, leaving him with only motivated troops and no infrastructure or paraphernalia to command. So, with our raising team, we embarked on a journey to build everything from scratch. Surprisingly, every day ended with a sense of achievement and pride, despite the initial lack of established infrastructure and resources.

One peculiar perk of being the "COW" was the luxury of having a trained chef at my disposal; but being a new raising, this was not to be the case for me! As someone who was known for culinary escapades and struggles, this was a hilarious twist of fate. No more cheesecakes, desserts, pies, or delicious continental cuisine: now, I was the troop tasked with training a chef. The excitement reached its peak when the

Adjutant informed me that a chef would be reporting at 10 am.

We welcomed Sepoy Manoj with open arms, but just as we settled into the routine, he went on leave after three months. Enter Sepoy Manoj Jawale. Just as we thought we had everything figured out with dinners and visits, three months flew by, and Manoj was ready for his leave. This time, however, I realised Sheri had given instructions for the chefs cooking for the troops to be trained under me to become special Officers' Mess chefs.

Poor me, indeed. Well, that third time turned out to be the charm – or rather, the last laugh.

As I recall the events leading up to Sheri's move to Umroi, a small place on the way to Shillong in the northeast (Meghalaya) of India, I could not help but feel a mixture of emotions. Life had come full circle. As if Sheri was getting posted to places where I had been with papa.

On one hand, I was filled with pride and happiness for Sheri as he was about to embark on the journey of raising a battalion. It was like being a parent all over again, assuming the responsibilities of a senior spouse, a role filled with endless work, being looked up to, countless sleepless nights, and a never-ending schedule of travel. However, I also could not deny the feeling of insecurity that both mothers were no doubt experiencing, as they adjusted to the changes brought on by this new chapter in Sheri's life.

On a lighter note, as our family continued to grow, Jaskirat, our growing young son, began requesting a companion.

While having another sibling may have been a difficult proposition, we decided that the perfect solution was to bring a pet into our home. This led us to Amigo, a magnificent pedigree dog who was as calm in temperament as he was serene in behaviour. Kirat, our son, affectionately referred to him as "*mera bhai*," which means "my brother" in Punjabi. Amigo was truly a delight for all dog lovers and brought so much joy and comfort to our home, so, he was lovingly referred to as Amigo ji.

It's interesting to note how, in India, dogs are often referred to with a term of respect, like "*Ji*" which is often used as a suffix for addressing a person with the highest respect. This cultural quirk adds to the humour in the exchange and highlights the unique ways in which different culture's view and treat their pets. In many cultures across the world, pets hold a special place in people's hearts and are often considered a part of the family. In India, this bond is particularly strong, and dogs are often seen as protectors and guardians of the family. It was a delight to see how Amigo had become an integral part of our family, and how he had brought us all closer together.

As I walked with Amigo one evening, I overheard a conversation taking place behind me. "Who is this Mem Saab?" one person asked. To which the other replied with a chuckle, "I don't know who the lady is, but the dog is definitely my Commanding Officers'!" The humour in the exchange made me smile, as Amigo was not just any ordinary dog, but a dignified and elegant Basset Hound, befitting a Commanding Officer, commanding respect from all. This conversation reflected the bond I shared with Amigo and the love and admiration he commanded from those around us.

Kirat had fondly adopted Amigo as his younger brother. It was during an incident that involved the Hush Puppy going missing, and the entire station was searching for the Commanding Officers' dog. We had a small slushy lake in front of our appointment house, and there was fear that he might have fallen into it. After an unfruitful attempt to locate him, we had to inform little Kirat about our concern. Kirat thought for a while and exclaimed, "What if he reached the Assam regiment? Would he have been gobbled up?" On a lighter note, eventually, the Hush Puppy was found locked in the garage, hiding under the car. It was a search that turned out to be hilariously amusing.

Thereafter, Amigo was given a bell on his collar to ensure his silence could be tracked. Much to ease, the frantic search operations that happened frequently.

On some occasions, we had 14 officer families posted together, with the tremendous responsibility of creating a cohesive team. Many of these families had never served together before, and some were newly married. As a young Captain's wife, life was carefree, and I simply went along with what others did. But as time passed, the role became more structured, and I gracefully embraced my dual responsibility of looking after my extended army family.

The camaraderie among the ladies played a crucial role in our ability to take care of our soldiers' families. We understood and supported each other; the empathy making us a strong and united team, admired by others in the station.

I never felt pressured to answer anyone else in this role. There were times when the decisions were entirely in my hands, and I learned to take ownership of them. With time, we developed strong bonds and found ourselves striking similar chords, forming a tight-knit team.

Sheri, as always, was there to guide me through the difficulties I faced. He believed in balancing work and fun, following the motto that "all work and no play made Jack a dull boy". So, we made sure that our troops and officers took time off to unwind and have some fun.

During this period, we had this gang of newly commissioned officers in the new raising, and let me tell you, Shillong was like the irresistible charmer of the Northeast, pulling in the youngsters every weekend on their trusty motorbikes. Well, one day, the thrill got the better of them, and we had one of them ending up with a fractured leg, thanks to some overenthusiastic speeding around those twisty mountain roads. Ah, the perils of trying to make it to the fashion capital of the East in one piece!

Then there was this other officer, who decided to add a romantic twist to their escapades. Picture this – one officer, one girlfriend, and a grand elopement plan. It was like a Bollywood movie in the making, right in the middle of our officer shenanigans.

Fast forward a few years, and it hits me – all those mishaps were like our crash course in life's little lessons. Welcoming the newlyweds into our chaotic fold felt like déjà vu, only this time, I was on the other side of the aisle. The arrival of a newbie or an officer's spouse was like reliving the whole exciting journey.

Looking back, it is amazing how those fractured bones and elopements paved the way for some priceless wisdom. Life's a journey, my friend, and sometimes, you've got to speed through the curves and elope to truly appreciate the hilarity of it all.

SERENDIPITOUS SENTINALS

One memorable outing was when we planned a trip to Cherrapunji. We all travelled together on a bus, enjoyed adventurous activities, and shared laughter and meals as one big family. When we returned, a busload of us went for a cup of coffee, while a few officers chose not to join in. The complete bus landed upon return at the absent officer's residence, who had chosen not to accompany for a cup of coffee. It became a light-hearted incident, and we joked that the next time we planned an outing, no one would dare stay back.

The role of the "COW," proved to be a uniquely challenging yet immensely fulfilling responsibility, especially in the context of our newly raised unit. I envisioned my role as that of a mentor tasked with shaping a group of young women from diverse backgrounds, some of whom were unfamiliar with military culture and traditions, into mature and responsible military spouses. It was a delicate balancing act, requiring me to guide them without being overly pushy or overbearing, mindful of the generation gap and the perception of senior ladies from my own earlier days. Initially daunting, I took the plunge, realizing that achieving this task was possible if approached with passion, love, and fairness. During the change, I discovered wings I never knew I had. Before I knew it, we evolved into a happy and motivated family, proud of raising our baby regiment and bound together for life.

Kiran: The Ray of
Inspiration

Embarking on a reflective journey through the chapters of my life, it is imperative to pay tribute to the exceptional woman who profoundly shaped my existence—my beloved mother, Kanwal Kiran, fondly known as Gogi to her near and dear ones. Her life's narrative, intricately woven with the threads of the military, bore witness to the trials of an Army Kid and Bride, leaving an enduring imprint on my character.

Even the names Gonu and Gini bear the heartwarming imprint of our parents' endearing monikers. Derived from the affectionate terms "Noni" for papa and "Gogi" for Mummy, these names become not just labels but vibrant expressions of the unique and cherished relationships within our family. It's a beautiful reminder that our identities are intricately woven into the rich fabric of our family history, where even the simplest of names carry the weight of love, laughter, and the enduring ties that bind us together.

Kiran, the eldest among three sisters born to the respected Lt Col Prahlad Singh Sethi and Mrs Gurdip Sethi, emerged from a military lineage rooted in Gujjar Khan and Rawal Pindi, Pakistan. The crucible of their family's experiences during the tumultuous partition era instilled in them values of love, affection, correct mentorship, and the essence of a military upbringing. Notably, each sister chose life partners from the Army, Air Force, and Navy, epitomizing a truly Tri-Service family.

Upon reflection on the years spent with my mother, her exceptional nature becomes increasingly evident. Beyond being a devoted mother and caring daughter, Kiran possessed a unique gift—the ability to radiate warmth, fostering enduring friendships. Her boundless empathy consistently prioritised others over herself, making her an unwavering pillar of support for my infantryman father and our entire family. I aspire to emulate this remarkable quality, rooted in her positive approach to navigating adversity with an indomitable spirit.

While fulfilling the role of a contented homemaker, Kiran's artistic prowess as a creative designer illuminated our home, whether permanent, temporary, or makeshift bashas. Her flower arrangements, in particular, were nothing short of spectacular, leaving an indelible impression. The inheritance of this talent by Gini and me fills us with immense pride.

Let us delve into anecdotes that illuminate her extraordinary motherly instincts, extending beyond her children. Kiran found joy in guiding younger military spouses, offering solace and support. One poignant memory stands out from an Officers' Mess party when a young newlywed wife experienced a breakdown. Kiran's special effort to reach out, and bring her home, exemplified her compassionate nature. Always full of regimental spirit (typical *fauji* terminology for camaraderie), she made it a point to either host at home and if that was not possible due to the travellers' plans, carry a packed meal for any known family passing through our place of residence – a ritual she did not break till her last day, while papa was in service or even after his superannuation.

Her compassion and empathy were not limited to the *fauji* circles alone. After papa's retirement, they finally settled down at Defence Colony, New Delhi, an expensive neighbourhood of the national capital where commercialism takes priority over everything else. Unlike life in a military cantonment where everything was on call, one had to fend for daily needs from the nearby Central Market at Lajpat Nagar requiring a frequent commute. As she did not know how to drive and hiring a dedicated chauffeur was not economically viable, I often wondered how she would manage without papa's help. I was pleasantly surprised when I visited her. Would you believe it, she had a private *rikshawala* at her disposal who would pick her up from home, take her shopping from place to place, and wait patiently outside the shop or place of work, sometimes for the entire day and then drop her home. All this was not because she could afford to pay him an astronomical remuneration, but because she was kind, empathetic, and considerate. As I spent some more days with her at Defence Colony, I learned that this special service was not limited to the rickshaw (Tuk-Tuk) alone, she had an army of happy and willing service providers.

No wonder, she was always networked and resourceful, ensuring a foolproof ecosystem for survival, with or without and sometimes, despite the man of the house!

Her dedication as the familial pivot during the trials of Army life in the 70s, 80s, and 90s remains a testament to her strength. Separations, limited resources which included meagre salaries and the absence of readily available support systems did not dampen our upbringing. Kiran's resilience and smiling demeanour ensured our lives were characterised by abundance and joy. Never were these shortfalls of resources allowed to affect our upbringing and happiness. For us as children, we were living lives of royalty and everything the universe had to offer was at our disposal. All this was possible because Mummy was always in control and that too with a smiling face. She was also very much conscious of the fact that in our small nuclear family, papa was the only male member – for that matter even in the extended family from the maternal side, the situation was similar. This made her stronger and made it her mission to get the absolute best for her family. To achieve this, she developed patience and hard work, tried to attract new friends wherever we went, and learnt to work on making relationships last – even mending them whenever required. While she was a qualified and creatively gifted designer, she chose not to pursue it as a profession. Instead, she would be at the centre of any ladies' activity in the unit or a station, be it event management, mentorship or simply interaction with the jawans' families. This made her a true ambassador of human values while endearing her to one and all. As a consequence, even to this day - it's been more than a decade after she left, I have met so many people, both acquaintances and strangers whose lives were touched by her kindness and who remember her with fondness and respect. A legacy anyone would die for!

Even after papa's retirement, her support remained unwavering. Papa was a person of action and loved being in the driver's seat; he couldn't have asked for a better co-pilot! She knew that a typical retired life of relaxing at home garnished with long walks at dawn and dusk interspersed with a little socializing would not work for him. So, when he was chosen as the Head of a security firm running operations in Nepal, she was quick to pack her bags and accompany him. Later when he decided to return and pursue other passions and talents as an administrator and chief of marketing in an aviation company, she understood that he was getting to spread his wings and was happy to allow him space to fly. On her part, she immersed herself in doing what she enjoyed most, anchoring the family from D-328 Defence Colony. Nana – Nani by now were in their eighties, her two sisters were still not over with their domestic responsibilities, the circumstances were exactly right, and mummy assumed control. As she anchored the family from D 328 Defence Colony, her commitment to her parents in their eighties was truly inspirational.

Her captivating charm went beyond her achievements; what truly endeared her to everyone was her selfless ability to revel in and celebrate the successes of others. In a world often marked by competition and individual pursuits, she stood out as a beacon of genuine joy for the accomplishments of those around her. Whether it was a colleague's promotion, a friend's achievement, or a family member's milestone, her infectious enthusiasm and sincere congratulations created a supportive and uplifting atmosphere. Her altruistic spirit not only made her a cherished friend and ally but also left an indelible mark on the hearts of those fortunate enough to share in the glow of her warm and generous applause for the triumphs of others.

The full extent of Kiran's devotion became apparent when, despite battling Carcinoma detected in 2005, she steadfastly tended to her obligations. Her quiet and fuss-free approach to undergoing treatment revealed a strength that resonates deeply. When her condition improved and she went into remission after a yearlong treatment, she quickly bounced back to her childlike self which revelled in celebrating life. She utilised this extra lease of life to bask in the success and love of her children and grandchildren and travel long distances to Shillong and even Melbourne to meet me and Gini respectively. Alas! this recovery was short lived, and cancer struck again, this time even more aggressively five years later in 2009.

In the face of the sobering news and the discomfort of treatment, she displayed an unwavering determination to cling to her zest for life. Despite grappling with the challenges of her health, she remained a beacon of positivity, seamlessly executing her role as a perfect spouse. Not one to burden others with her struggles, she chose to shield Gini and me from the gravity of her situation, allowing us to focus on our own responsibilities. Her strength reached new heights when she not only motivated fellow patients facing similar battles but also took the bold step of sharing her journey on television. It was in those moments that the true warrior within her emerged, fighting tenaciously until the very end. Her resilience and selflessness became a source of inspiration, leaving an indelible mark on all who witnessed her courageous battle.

In commemorating Kanwal Kiran, we celebrate not only a life well-lived but an enduring legacy of kindness, empathy, and resilience. Her impact on countless lives, within and beyond military circles, paints a portrait of a woman whose influence transcends time—a legacy anyone would be honoured to inherit. A true testament to her character, she exemplified calmness and composure, notably in an incident where a competitor, during an event, hid her masterpiece in a corner. Despite the urging of others to confront the individual, Kiran chose grace over confrontation and, to everyone's surprise, received a well-deserved appreciation for her work. Her unwavering poise in the face of such a situation is a poignant reflection of her character—a woman of quiet strength and dignity. True to her name, Kiran was, and remains, a radiant and enduring source of inspiration.

Secunderabad Express – Journeying Through 2011

Kiran's untimely passing shook us. Time and tide stood for no one, but the show must go on. After a two-year stay at Umroi; it was time to move to Delhi again. This layover was less than a year. Sheri's nomination for another prestigious career course came as a welcome surprise, giving us hope of spending time with friends and reconnecting acquaintances.

The short but eventful stay at Secunderabad in Andhra Pradesh was yet another colourful chapter in our life as we moved there for a yearlong official training (Higher Defence Management Course) after short innings in Delhi. This bustling city, which is one of the six zones of the Greater Hyderabad Municipal Corporation, is a hub of activity and new experiences.

During our stay here, I made many new friends, reconnected with old coursemates, and formed lasting bonds. The time spent there was filled with fun, laughter, plenty of shopping, and travel. It was a magical time in my life. The unique blend of old friendships and new experiences, combined with the rich cultural heritage of India, made Secunderabad special. Even though short tenures gave us time to unwind from our tough long tenures where you only focus on professional tasks assigned. Contrary to that, the officers get a chance to become students, attend classes, and sometimes get involved in domestic and international educational travels.

During my stay there, I had the pleasure of rekindling old friendships with many of my friends (Anu, Sonu, Sweety, Nanu, Mannu, Shikha, Simmi, Namita, Vibha, Shalu, Neetu, and Meena to name a few Karma sisters). One of them became my next-door neighbour, Soni Sangwan. Soni who was a well-known journalist, visited me during our tenure in Shillong a couple of years ago. She had even served as a news commentator during the Kargil War, making her an accomplished and fascinating person to be around. Her adorable daughter, Sona, was the highlight of my days, as the little girl was always either at our place or I was at their place. Every morning we were the familiar faces we would open our doors to.

As the days went by, I noticed that my dog, Amigo, had developed a peculiar habit. Whenever our husbands would leave for their classes, Amigo would disappear. It wasn't until later that I discovered Amigo was ready and waiting outside Soni's home, eagerly awaiting the eight egg yolks that were discarded by Colonel Sandeep, affectionately referred to as "Sandy" by Soni.

Wherever you would see a group of children, Saint Amigo had to be in the centre; he became the hot favourite amongst the children on the course. And our identity was that of Amigo's mummy papa.

Now, let's talk about our adorable little Kirat – the 'Prince of snacks and sweets.' This boy had a knack for surviving on snacks and sweets. If it were up to him, he'd live on chips and candies all day long! But of course, as the self-proclaimed supermom, I was determined to change that. I took it upon myself to stuff him with all the healthy goodies I could find. You name it, and I tried it! Fruits, vegetables, whole grains – they were all part of my strategy to transform Kirat into a healthy eating machine. I'd concoct many creative dishes, hoping that he would gobble them up with delight. But alas, it seemed like my efforts often ended up in disappointment. Kirat would simply give me that adorable, innocent look as if to say, "Thanks, Mommy, but I'll pass."

It was like a never-ending battle of wills at the dining table. I'd come up with fun names for the dishes, play airplane games with the spoon, and even tell silly stories to distract him from the taste of vegetables. But it seemed like he had a secret superpower to detect any trace of "healthy" in his food. Despite all the struggles, I never gave up. I was determined.

Oh, the banana saga during Kirat's daily walks to the school bus was quite an amusing experience. It all started innocently enough - as a daily ritual, I'd hand him a banana to munch on during his walk. I thought it would be a nutritious snack to keep him energised throughout the day. But then, enter my friend Soni with her sage advice. She had this sneaky suspicion that something fishy was going on with those bananas. So, we played detective and followed Kirat one morning.

And what did we find? Kirat, the little trickster, was secretly sharing his banana feast with the neighbourhood strays! He had become the banana supplier to all the street dogs around. Now, you'd think Amigo, our furry friend, might have had something to say about this. But nope, he was as cool as ever, amused by the whole situation. After all, who wouldn't enjoy a banana, treat occasionally?

So, there we were, feeling like we had cracked some major case, only to discover that both Amigo and the stray dogs were in on this banana conspiracy together. It was like they had formed an unspoken alliance, united by their love for this fruit. Who knew that a simple banana could become the centerpiece of a grand canine snack distribution scheme?

Sheri, in his infinite wisdom, had all
the time in this world to focus on
polishing his Game of Golf.
He also had this bright idea
to teach me how to drive a
car. I must admit, I was dead
set on learning through a
professional driving school. You know how it is, right? When
husbands try to teach their spouses to drive a car, there is often
chaos! So, Sheri and I embarked on this driving adventure,
and it was quite a spectacle. Sheri tried to stay patient while I
struggled with the basics of driving. It didn't take long for us
to realise that this would not work out.

In a moment of defeat, we both surrendered and decided to
join a driving school. So off we went, signing up for proper
driving lessons. I thought this would be a significant change
and that I'd soon be cruising the streets with confidence.
Well, let me tell you, even after all those hours of instruction
and practice, I still couldn't drive to save my life! It was like I
had a mental block or something. I did manage to get my
driver's license eventually, but in all honesty, I think they gave
it to me out of pity.

But you know what? I wasn't too disheartened about it. I
passionately believe that everything happens at its own time
and pace. Maybe driving just wasn't my forte at that moment,
and that was okay. Looking back, those were some
unforgettable times. Sheri may not have been an expert
driving instructor, but we had a good laugh about it all. And
hey, who knows? One day, when the stars align exactly right,

I'll surprise everyone and become the smoothest driver around! Until then, my case rests.

Most of us had kids of similar age groups and it was a big reunion of old friends. Our days were filled with laughter and adventures. We had all the facilities, a football ground, a basketball court- you name it. But the real action happened in the middle of the campus. There was a small little grocery shop in the middle of the campus. Now this grocery store wasn't an ordinary one. It was a magical place that sold the most mind-blowing ice cream you could imagine. And let me tell you, it had a gravitational pull that attracted swarms of children at all hours. Even my furry friend Amigo knew exactly where to park himself after his daily walks, hoping for a heavenly ice cream.

Amidst all this and indulgence in ice cream, the mothers were secretly plotting to get in shape for the upcoming foreign tour. Oh, the fitness frenzy was something to behold. We would gather at the Gym, pretending to exercise, but it was more of a comedy show. We'd be panting and gasping for breath and after a few moments of planning our post-tour escapades. "Those were the days, my friend." The Dhruva enclave was our little Paradise filled with laughter and camaraderie.

During our stay, we were presented with an excellent opportunity — an opportunity to travel abroad on a study tour. We got ours to the land Down Under, Australia! Our mission: to explore the dazzling cities of Sydney, Canberra, and Melbourne. But before I dive into our Aussie adventure, let me paint you a picture of what happened on the home front.

Picture this: mothers frantically packing their kids into a safe zone like it was some top-secret mission. Grandparents swooping in to save the day and to babysit. Some brave mothers, with little ones in tow, had to stay behind. But these unsung heroes volunteered to watch over the kiddos left behind, turning our campus into a makeshift daycare. Kirat, however was lucky. Since papa had travel plans to Melbourne, he got to travel with him almost one month before our scheduled trip.

Let's get back to the travel shenanigans! Our journey kicked off at Hyderabad Airport. We had a brief pit stop in Thailand before we could finally shout "G'day!" to Sydney. In the land of kangaroos and koalas, our days were a rollercoaster of official meetings and touristy escapades.

The journey from Sydney to Canberra was a road trip for the ages, spanning two scenic days. We even made a pit stop in Boral, a quaint town with a museum dedicated to none other than Sir Don Bradman, the cricket legend.

Canberra was up next, and it had a unique twist waiting for us – a War Memorial Service. Families of fallen soldiers were the stars of the show, and the names of the heroes echoed through the air. The vibe in Canberra had a touch of Chandigarh in it, surprisingly. And oh, we couldn't miss the Flower Festival Floriade, a cultural fiesta where tradition, art, and craft mingled beautifully. A trip to Red Hill, the highest peak, was all about spotting kangaroos in their element.

Then came the pièce de resistance — Melbourne! Our hearts soared as we embarked on the Great Ocean Drive. Towns like

Torquay, Apollo Bay, Lorne, and Port Campbell flaunted views that could make anyone's jaw drop. But the highlight? A helicopter ride over the Twelve Apostles. Our cameras had never worked so hard! This trip was like a masterclass in globetrotting and embracing diverse cultures. Our treasure trove of memories from Australia was filling up fast.

On our last official day in Melbourne, Daljit, my brother-in-law, came to pick us up for the three-day holiday that followed the study tour. We made our way to Gini's home nestled far from the CBD, where papa, Kirat, and her kids, Jaskaran and Jaskabeer, welcomed us with open arms. The kids had bonded like lifelong pals during our absence, and the three days that followed were a whirlwind of sightseeing, picnics, and quality family time.

Back home, the tour didn't end just yet. We had a holiday in Thailand, and Kirat joined us there. Kirat had spent over a month with his cousins, and the emotional farewell was heart-wrenching. But Thailand was a different ballgame – group tours, shopping sprees, and touristy hotspots. Some moms who'd stayed back because of their little ones finally got to reunite with their husbands and kids. The highlight? Mrs Pannu, our superhero senior, brought six kids on the flight to meet their parents abroad, proving once again that we were one big, chaotic family.

When we returned, life resumed to its usual rhythm. Ladies fell back to their daily routines, officers went back to their classrooms, and the kids marched back to school. After all, vacations can't last forever.

Amidst all this, doctors dropped some tough news. They advised us to stop Kuki's chemotherapy and focus on giving her the best quality of life. It was gut-wrenching but necessary. To make things easier, we invited them to stay with us, as it had become challenging for Kuki to run her household.

And that wasn't the only big news on the horizon. In Delhi, my father, Mahip papa, reached a significant milestone – he wrote his first book, "Grit Guts and Gallantry." It was a shining moment in his life since the loss of my mother. After Kiran's passing, he found solace in writing and penned five books. His rocky journey with his first publisher eventually led to the birth of Creative Crows Publishers LLP, where he aimed to support budding authors in achieving their publishing dreams. Along with his partner, Tannaaz Irani, they had dived headfirst into the world of publishing. Mahip papa shared the exciting progress of Creative Crows Publishers LLP with me, and he expressed his deep desire for me to join the team. We experienced a profound sense of elation as our father finally uncovered his true calling.

This story, with all its ups, downs, and unexpected turns, celebrates the resilience of the human spirit, the power of determination, and the strength of a supportive community. It's like a modern-day Phoenix rising from the ashes, proving that even in the face of adversity, we can find our purpose and soar to new heights. Cheers to life's unpredictable journey!

Narangi Chronicles – Assam 2012 Edition

B idding adieu to Secunderabad, we waited for our epic travels to begin again. As we embarked on our next assignment to Guwahati in the North-East of India, Kuki, and papa were our companions. Memories of my childhood came alive, the green state, the tea gardens, and the inviting people. Only this time, Sheri's parents accompanied us instead of my parents. Kuki now required medical attention more frequently than before. The pain had become unbearable, and it was no longer possible to care for her at home in Patiala. We were in search of a place to stay that was closer to a hospital so that we could easily attend to Kuki's needs. So, we parked ourselves in Narangi Cantt Guwahati.

Meanwhile, Sheri assumed his assignments in the remote locales of Assam. Knowing that his mother and family were in a place of safety, he could prioritise his attention on the new challenges placed upon him. The great attraction for us back in Narangi was that the campus had the necessities and Kirat's school was also just a few minutes away. The house had an elephant track next to my bedroom window, and we had been briefed that in case of a crossing, we had to remain quiet and turn the light off. Quite an interesting enthralling event for little Kirat. Adding to this epic adventure, we had a group of naughty monkeys picking the neighbours' clothes every day, but it went to greater lengths when one of them choose to do a dance performance with her dupatta. In no time, we were trying to distract her to give away her piece of clothing.

Kuki's health deteriorated as time moved. She would get intense pain and pain administration became a necessity. During our search, we were blessed to discover a Palliative Care team in Guwahati who offered their support and expertise in pain management. This compassionate and dedicated team provided much-needed comfort and relief during her difficult time. Their commitment to providing quality care to those in need was truly inspiring.

This experience highlights the key role that Palliative Care Teams play in improving the quality of life for those facing serious illnesses. It was a humbling reminder of the power of compassion and the impact it can have on someone's life. In many countries around the world, the act of caring for those in need is a sacred duty, and the work of Palliative Care Teams is a testament to this cultural value.

The journey with Kuki had been a roller coaster ride, filled with both ups and downs. Despite the challenges, she remained steadfast in her faith, drawing strength from her religious beliefs. This devotion to her faith was evident in the hospice she chose to spend her few days in a convent run by kind-hearted nuns who provided her with comfort and care. Though a practitioner of Sikhism, Kuki's faith was deeply influenced by the Bible she had imbibed during her days of teaching in a convent, and it was no surprise that she felt a sense of peace being surrounded by the sisterhood at the convent.

It was a challenging time for all of us, but we tried to make the best of the situation by being there for her and providing her with the support she needed. Despite the pain she was experiencing, Kuki remained strong, never losing sight of her belief that healing would eventually come.

Eventually, the time came when Kuki's condition worsened, and we had to move her to the ICU in the hospital. The three days that followed were a flurry of difficulties, and I knew the end was near. I urged Sheri to return as soon as possible, knowing that our world was slipping away.

Kuki passed away peacefully, surrounded by her loved ones, her last wish of being close to her children fulfilled. Her life was a fulfilling one, spent caring for her family, grandchildren, and children. Her ashes were finally immersed in the mighty Brahmaputra close to the highly revered deity

Maa Kamakhya Devi, a symbol of her life well lived. The memories of her kindness, her strength, and her unwavering faith will remain with us forever.

Losing two loved ones within just three years is a tough journey for anyone to endure, especially for two elderly fathers who have been used to having their wives by their side for decades. However, both men displayed immense strength and courage as they learned to navigate life without the women who had been the centre of their world for so long.

Mahip papa channelled his grief into writing and published a book about his experiences as a widower. 'HE ME & SHE' is full of humour and laughter and is a rib-tickling read, replete with light-hearted moments. He was able to find solace in the company of his grandchildren, his colleagues, travels, a good game of golf, and his publishing house. While he would sometimes miss his wife, he never wallowed in self-pity and always kept himself busy with meaningful activities.

Gurdip papa, on the other hand, found comfort in the quiet of libraries and long walks. He could come to terms with his loss and find a new purpose in life. He was eventually able to travel to San Francisco to visit his daughter Rohini and her family, including the newest addition to their family, baby Aayan, his third grandchild. In his role as a doting grandfather, he could provide care and support to the little one during this special time.

Both fathers serve as a testament to the resilience and strength of the human spirit. Despite losing their partners, they were able to adapt and find joy in life once again. It is a reminder that, like the cycles of nature, life goes on, and there is always hope for happiness in the future.

We moved in with Sheri at his location at Rangia. He had a charming little standalone home. Amigo would bask in the sun all day. Kirat joined the school which was run by our organisation. I too followed suit by uniting with him there as the Principal. This opportunity gave me a chance to consolidate all my learnings in one place. So much could be done for the betterment of the next generation through fusion of culture and education. I shared my vision with the personnel, and they were more than eager to participate in bringing about the change. The campus was so small that we could do a tour of the camp in 15 minutes. Life taught us to live with bare necessities and fewer expectancies. It was a tremendously busy time for Sheri, for he was frequently travelling around. We didn't realise that 8 months passed so swiftly. The sudden news of Sheri's transfer, once again to Delhi, was both a welcome surprise and a shock. Hoping to have a slight permanence in our next tenure, we marched forward toward our new destination.

Rediscovering Delhi –
The Years 2014-17

Our work had us relocated to Delhi from Assam. Ah, Delhi, the city of challenges and adventures! We faced the infamous accommodation shortage, moving from one house to another, like nomads, in search of our perfect home. It was like playing house-hunting roulette, but finally, after experiencing (South Extension, Battle Honours Mess, Mahip papa's house, and hostel accommodation) and eight months into our tenure, we settled into our dream home, which felt like a victory monument. And that's the beauty of life – it takes us on unexpected journeys, with twists and turns that shape us into stronger, more resilient individuals. Delhi brought its share of challenges, but it also gifted us with growth, new opportunities, and a place to call our own.

After a year of being settled in the city, our family decided it was time for a well-deserved break. Our destination of choice was Dubai, a city renowned for its luxurious amenities and exhilarating adventures. Our family, comprising my husband, Jaskirat, our son, and I, set out for a four-day trip filled with excitement and bonding opportunities.

One of the first activities on our itinerary was conquering dunes in a four-wheeled beast, which made me question whether I was on vacation or auditioning for a role in a Middle Eastern version of Mad Max. My curly, frizzy hair trying to escape the confines of a mandatory headscarf, and my face contorted into a mix of terror and exhilaration with every dune we conquered. This adventure was not my cup of tea, but I didn't want to become a spoilsport.

After surviving the desert rollercoaster, we thought, why not trade in the sand for a more liquid landscape? So, we hopped on a river cruise that was the nautical equivalent of a magic carpet ride. As the sun set, Dubai's skyline lit up like a futuristic disco, proving that this city is more than just skyscrapers and luxury shopping – it's also got a flair for dramatic lighting. The sun was setting as we sailed along the river, and the city came alive with its stunning skyline and illuminated buildings. It was a reminder of how diverse and beautiful the world can be.

Next, we drove onto Ferrari World Abu Dabi, where the need for speed met the desire for theme park thrills. My husband and son decided to tackle the highest-loop roller coaster, leaving me to play the role of the concerned-but-not-so-brave cheerleader. It was like watching a live-action drama where the plot twist was whether they'd regret their life choices or emerge with adrenaline-fuelled grins. Spoiler alert: they chose the latter, and I learned that Dubai's idea of family bonding involves defying gravity together. Who needs trust falls when you can have loop-the-loops?

Our trip to Dubai was a much-needed break from our daily lives, spending quality time together. The memories we created during our four days in Dubai will last a lifetime. We returned to Delhi feeling revived and reinvigorated.

A few months later, I got a call from my bestie Soni Sangwan, stirring up memories from our good old Hyderabad days. Soni and I have this timeless connection that defies the constraints of time and space. She's not just a friend; she's my lifeline, my partner in crime, and the one who makes my life hilariously bearable. Our friendship is like a fine wine – it only gets better with time. No matter how long it's been since our last chat, the moment Soni's voice crackles through the phone, it's like we've been yapping away for hours. She's seen me through thick and thin, from my triumphant victories to my epic failures.

Amid our laughter-filled catch-up, Soni threw a curveball at me – an all-women trip to Bali and Malaysia. Now, the idea of travelling with a pack of unknown ladies initially sounded like a plot twist from a suspense thriller. But channelling my inner daredevil, I took Sheri's advice and he blurted out a resounding "yes" without a second thought. What followed was a wild 10-day escapade with 10 ladies of different age groups venturing through the tropical wonders of Bali and Malaysia. Bali, the Indonesian gem, welcomed us with its cultural richness, warm vibes, and beaches that would make any sun worshipper do a happy dance.

Our days were filled with frolicking on the beaches of Nusa Dua, Seminyak, and Kuta – sun-soaked perfection. Ubud, with its mesmerising rice terraces and cliff-perched temples, was like stepping into a postcard. And oh, the Kecak fire dance against the backdrop of a Bali sunset – it was so enchanting that even the rain had to take a backseat.

For organised tours, shopping is like a military operation. But Soni and I, the rebels of the group, pulled a stunt during our Mount Batur return. We did a guerrilla-style stop and snagged some locally handcrafted souvenirs, much to the dismay of our tour operator. Oops!

Then came Malaysia, where we explored like there was no tomorrow. The Twin Towers watched over us as we chowed down on an evening feast. The Batu Caves left us in awe, but nothing could top the chocolate coma we slipped into at the jaw-dropping chocolate museum. And Soni, ever the explorer, pitched the idea of hitting up The Royal Selangor Pewter factory – because who doesn't want to see the world's fourth precious metal, right?

But what truly made the trip legendary were the fantastic ladies we shared it with. Each day is etched in my memory like a comedy show – full of laughter, unexpected twists, and a sprinkle of chaos. As I reminisce about this uproarious adventure, it's clear that travel has this magical power to bring people from all walks of life together. Age is just a number, and we proved that, uniting to soak in the joy of new experiences and create a treasure trove of memories.

Ah, life has a funny way of surprising us! By 2014, I had transformed into a total homebody, and Mummy's absence had left me feeling a bit laid back. But leave it to Sheri to shake things up! He came up with the brilliant idea of joining a fitness program nearby in Delhi, and though I was a tad reluctant at first, I decided to take on the challenge.

Guess what? I surprised myself! In no time, I transformed into a fitness pro, crunching away those kilos like a champ! I shed a whopping 13 kilos and felt on top of the world like I had conquered Everest (well, almost).

Feeling empowered and confident, I took on another challenge — applying for a job. And wouldn't you know it? I got the job in the blink of an eye! It was like the universe was aligning in my favour, cheering me on to achieve my goals.

Sheri remarked, if you want to work, learn to drive. And there I was, not only learning to drive but to drive to work at the age of forty-five. A feat I finally accomplished!

So, there I was, juggling my new job and fitness journey like a pro. But, as life often goes, time flew by, and my busy job eventually took over. The fitness journey slowly evaporated, like a bubble floating away, but it left me with a sense of accomplishment and happiness for all that I had achieved.

Working for Fabindia was a true milestone in my life. It all started in 2014 when I was offered the role of a Store Manager in one of their home stores in Gurgaon. At first, people were taken aback when they learned about my new position, often asking me about my qualifications and what my role entailed.

As a Store Manager, I was responsible for managing the day-to-day operations of the store, interacting with customers, promoting sales, and meeting targets. And let me tell you, those were some of the most fulfilling years of my life. I discovered a newfound confidence and contentment as I embraced this new chapter in my life. I was made responsible for my team of eleven young boys and girls, the responsibility of the upkeep of the interiors. Meeting targets became the work of my left hand as I have been blessed with the gift of gab. Ultimately, customers became friends and friends became customers. I give all the credit to the upbringing and the confidence instilled in us by our fraternity. Poor Sheri was always intimidated by the increasing number of Fabindia shopping bags that would land up at our home every fortnight. I was employed at shoppers' paradise and a house-proud woman within me knew no boundaries. All my hard-earned coupons would be spent on the first day itself. It was simply a habit I had to combat. Talk about working at a place where shopping is constantly on your mind, phew!

I worked with the brand of retail stores for a total of four years, and it was truly an amazing experience. From handling the reins of the store to evolving as a person, I am grateful for the memories and growth opportunities that working for Fabindia provided me. It's a testament to the power of stepping out of your comfort zone and trying something new, even at the age of forty-five. And as they say, you're never too old to learn new tricks. I would like to mention two fine ladies, Aarti and Anoora, who trusted me and let me lead the store with full integrity and ownership. I still remember them asking me in one interview about my biggest strength. Without a doubt, I answered my 'SMILE'.

A few months earlier, I had received a call from my father, who made me an offer I wasn't sure I could refuse. He wanted me to become his business partner and help him take his company to new heights. At first, I was flattered by the offer. But after giving it some thought, I had to decline. My job at Fabindia was becoming demanding, and I didn't want to risk doing a disservice to my father's hard work and dedication to his business.

To be honest, I also had concerns about the impact that working with my father might have on our relationship as father and daughter. I feared that the stress and pressures of working together might strain our bond and affect our cherished relationship.

However, as I look back on this offer from papa and my subsequent refusal, I reiterate that I do believe that unique challenges arise when family and work collide. It's a common scenario in many cultures around the world, where familial ties and obligations can often conflict with the demands of a career. But at the same time, there are many examples of families who have successfully navigated these waters and built successful businesses together.

With a bit of humour, I like to think of it as a classic case of "the family that works together, stays together". But in all seriousness, it surely is a balancing act that requires careful consideration, open communication, and a willingness to compromise. And who knows, one day we'll look back on this moment and laugh about how silly our worries were, just like the old joke about the family-owned hot-air balloon business: "We're going up, but we're not sure where we're headed!"

PART – III

A LIFETIME OF
WISDOM AND
RESILIENCE

From barracks to vows, my journey's spun,
a fauji brat to a spouse, battles won.
Learned discipline's dance, found purpose anew,
with confidence forged, a well-rounded view.

Mahip – The Avid Golfer and a Versatile Writer

During the last week of December 2016, I telephoned papa to receive a general update from him. He missed mummy, probably as he had just attended the funerals of two of his coursemates. He told me to keep a set of his house keys with me, in case something happened to him. I was initially upset, but he continued to tell me he had made his will and that he wanted to go with his last rites from the Barar Square (A crematorium that gives a befitting send-off to soldiers with full Military Honours). I had nothing to say, but yes. That was it.

The passing away of my beloved papa was a shock that shook my world to its core. One moment, he was playing a vigorous game of golf, showing his determination to finish all 18 holes, and the next moment he was gone from us, leaving us all in a state of disbelief. His dedication to his work was evident even on his last day as he finished editing his final book.

Papa lived a life that was full of adventure and purpose. He touched the lives of countless individuals, as evidenced by the outpouring of love and condolences that flooded my Facebook post announcing his passing. The sheer volume of messages that morning on his Facebook page, from friends, colleagues, followers, and family members, was a testament to the impact that papa had made during his time here on earth.

In many cultures, the passing of a loved one is seen as a time to celebrate their life and all the good they brought into the world. In the same vein, I choose to celebrate the incredible life that papa lived, full of passion and drive, right up until his final day. Although he may be gone from us physically, his spirit and influence will continue to live on in the memories and hearts of those who knew and loved him.

My father was a true perfectionist in every sense of the word. He was always meticulous in his planning and had a keen eye for detail. Even in his final days, he had planned for us to be taken care of after he was gone. He had stocked up on food for a whole month, made sure the groceries were in place, the cooking gas cylinders were full, and he even had cash in his wallet. It was as if he knew that my sister and I would be staying in his home after he left.

His final journey, which was a huge congregation of his well-wishers. It was poignant and heart-wrenching affair. As he was laid to rest at the Brar Square, the most fitting tribute to a soldier in life and death. It was a sombre affair, and it felt like the world was at a standstill in mourning.

Irony is a funny thing. Just a few days before he passed, both our fathers had been invited to a special ceremony where my husband Sheri was honoured with the prestigious Sena Medal. If only my father had been with us for just one more day, he would have had the chance to witness the event and see his son-in-law being honoured for his service to the nation.

My father was always eager to share his experiences from his time as an ex-NDA with anyone who would listen. He used to tell us about his weekends spent discussing common topics with other ex-servicemen. I used to tease him sometimes, asking what he would do if his son-in-law wasn't an Ex-NDA. With whom would he have shared his stories then? It's these moments of levity that keep us going, even in the darkest of times.

Indeed, papa was the liveliest person I have ever known...always bringing sunshine and happiness in whichever group he was. I think he is best described in his epitaph by Sheri, my husband and I quote: "Col Mahip Chadha, Gonu's dad, and my buddy is no more…just about coming to terms with the fact that a person so alive can also embrace death. But yes, his departure was so typically Mahip Chadha – 'I give a damn!' Played a wonderful round of 18 holes in the morning, worked on his latest book till late in the evening, and departed in his sleep, not allowing even death to shake him…that's Mahip Chadha for all of us to remember… A soldier, a golfer, an author, a philanthropist, and a zealous soul born to live and enjoy every moment of life. Papa, you may be gone in person, but your spirit is right here in the 'Mahipism' you leave behind with so many hearts that you have touched…I really don't know if you can RIP, as you weren't really the one made to rest, but continue to celebrate and spread happiness in your eternal afterlife!"

Creative Wings

After bidding farewell to my dear father, my partner in crime and convincer extraordinaire, Tannaaz Irani, entered the scene. She swooped down from Mumbai like a literary superhero, armed with charm and an unwavering determination to lure me into the world of Creative Crows Publishers – a legacy my father left for us to nurture.

At first, I was clinging to my Fabindia job like a koala on a eucalyptus tree. Steady salary, familiar surroundings – what more could a person want? But Tannaaz, with her persuasive powers, made me an offer I couldn't refuse. So, in February 2017, I traded my comfort zone for the unpredictable rollercoaster of publishing.

Our journey, my friends, was nothing short of an epic saga. We kicked off with a humble sixty titles, and now, we've got a library of two hundred and fifty books, spanning genres like a buffet at a literary feast. From authors aged 9 to those with a few more trips around the sun, we've got it all. Our social media game went from zero to hero, turning us into the Beyoncé of the publishing world. People often ask, "How on earth did you two pull this off?" Well, besides Tannaaz and me being a dynamic duo, I like to think it's the hard work, determination, and a sprinkle of divine guidance from my father, who's probably up there somewhere giving us a thumbs-up.

I inherited more than just my dad's knack for energy – I got the gift of gab and the enthusiasm to keep the Creative Crows flame burning bright. The idea for my venture, THE CROW'S LEGACY, popped into my head during one of my literary escapades to Pune. It's like my father's legacy got a makeover, and now it's rocking a new, vibrant energy. The thrilling journey kicks off right here in this document, folks. Stay tuned for the chaos and charm that ensued in the making of this legacy!

Phoren Lands

Buckle up for the most incredible family adventure ever! The summer of 2017 was all about promises and unforgettable memories. We had Rohini (Sheri's sister) waiting for us, and boy, did we turn it into an epic trip! Behind the scenes, tickets, visas, and the decision to visit her, and her family were more than overdue. I have always believed that distance is reduced if families keep meeting as much as possible. Technology has made it simpler with FaceTime and distances are just a state of mind but, in those days in the late 90s the situation was different. It had been almost 18 years since Rohini had moved to the USA. My mother-in-law's health had made her travel back more frequently. Honestly, on the lighter side, foreign travel requires a strong savings plan.

Our primary motive behind the travel along with the family reunion was acquainting Kirat with the foreign campuses, therefore our first stop was college hunting for Kirat. San Francisco had some interesting Art schools, campuses of Stanford, and Berkley were our major visiting goals. Thereafter, we packed ourselves in a hired Dodge Minivan. With Kirat in the rear with Rohinis five and three years old, poor Kirat was eventually buried under a sea of snacks and… spilled milk.? Of course, by the little kids. What a trooper! But hey, it was all part of the fun! Tall and grown-up, Kirat got some relief when Sheri took the wheel from Miguel. Ah, the joys of family road trips!

We hit the road and lived the dream in Las Vegas, the city of lights. Rohini had got an interesting deal to stay at the most attractive Paris Hotel. We spent the evening travelling through the strip, witnessing the musical fountain of Bellagio. The fireworks on the 4th of July lit up the city of Las Vegas. In the morning Sheri, Kirat, Miguel and I left the children behind and drove through the miles-long desert and what we saw, left us breathless "The majestic Grand Canyon." Cruising through LA visiting the famous Universal Studios, travelling on the streets of the city.

Upon reaching San Diego, Sheri decided he had to take the wheels. Suddenly, we heard the sirens behind us. It was the police. Miguel told Sheri to park the vehicle on one side. It turned out that Sheri had been driving without the headlights switched on; they asked him for his license and handed it over with a salute, acknowledging him as a uniformed officer. It was a startling revelation; Armed Forces were treated with the utmost respect everywhere in the world. The young officers even escorted us to the nearest highway out of the city. We were unstoppable in our thirst for adventure. But hold your hats, there's more! Off we went on an exciting journey to Lake Tahoe via Reno, where the sights were like something out of a fairytale. The exotic scenery of snowcapped mountains and the beautiful emerald colour lake was seen to be believed. To add to the fun were the beautiful, landscaped vineyards of the Napa Valley, the quaint tiny town of Sanoma also on the way, and "The Fifteen Mile drive" along with the" Pebble Beach" to "Carmel by the Sea"- the ultimate dream destination, even for the celebrities who live in Beverly Hills. Rohini ensured we had to touch every bit of history and adventure. Of course, we couldn't miss the iconic landmarks and breathtaking views of San Francisco. The drive on the Golden Gate Bridge is a celebration. Quite an achievement in a trip of a mere "twenty days."

Continuing the wheels of travels, 2018 had another surprise in store for us – Sheri's assignment to Hawaii! It was like stepping into a magical paradise, 2000 miles away from the mainland. Sheri came and announced that it was extremely short notice and that we had to travel on different itineraries. I was firm in my belief that if there was a will, there was a way. Though I couldn't join him on the same flight, I embarked on one of my first solo international travels. It went to Shanghai and then onward to Honolulu. I still managed to reach three hours ahead of his teammates and him. I found myself welcomed by local dancers swaying to the Ukulele tunes. I embraced the beauty of Hawaii and had breathtaking views while exploring the island.

During our time there, we embarked on a cruise that was the highlight of our trip. The beautiful Ala Moana area and the enchanting cruise left us in awe of Hawaii's splendour. The last day was devoted to an evening hosted by the team conducting the assignment. The social interaction with the officers made me realise the same joys of being a military spouse, serving your country, relocating with families, moving homes, and taking care of your subordinates were common across all armies. The evening was full of light-hearted interaction and great hospitality between the men in uniform.

Next morning, aligning ourselves with history we visited the historical military base, Pearl Harbour. A drive through the military base with a visit to witness the war museum and a solemn trip to the sunken USS Arizona were both emotional and educational experiences. It was a realisation that war has similar repercussions no matter which country encounters it.

On my return, I was scheduled for a layover in San Francisco while Sheri had to travel back to India. I stayed on and after meeting up with Rohini and her family; extending my trip. I travelled to Phoenix, where my cousin brother Sukrit and his wonderful wife Vinny, lived. It was a beautiful reunion and together we explored the local town in the evening, reminiscing about our childhood memories and getting to know his wife. Next morning, we drove to the captivating desert town of Sedona, surrounded by majestic red rock canyons. It was a trip filled with laughter and unforgettable moments.

I would like to talk about my experience of turbulence and long air travels – yikes! As a bit of a chicken, I'm always planning on how to survive any bumps. My prayers and countdown to touchdown become my trusted companions, helping me stay calm. But you know what puts me at ease? The looks on the flight attendants' faces! I follow the mantra "Keep calm if the attendant is calm." And with Sheri by my side, I feel reassured, knowing he's always cool and composed. So, fellow adventurers, how do you handle turbulence during flights? Share your secrets as we continue this incredible journey called life. Safe travels and happy landings to all of you – may each trip be filled with laughter, love, and unforgettable experiences.

Jodhpur Calling – Embrace the Royalty – 2018

Sheri and I had grown up in these past golden years and the realisation swept in when he was tasked with taking on larger roles as soon as we returned from our official assignment to Hawaii. With a promotion, we stood posted to Jodhpur in Rajasthan. Jaskirat was in the final years of his schooling. He had no choice but to stay in Delhi, a choice any child of his age would love to make. Away from the prying eyes of his parents and friends at his disposal.

Life in Jodhpur was bustling with activity, especially with Sheri's professional commitments. We were mesmerised by the stunning Umaid Palace that overlooked the golf course near our home. The colourful markets, filled with a variety of food options like *Lal Maas, Palak ke Chaat, and Dal Bhati Choorma, Kachauris stuffed with onions, lentils (red meat, lentils, lentil fritters and sweet)* were a food lover's paradise. We made many new friends who came to visit us, including tourists who were passing through, and our stay in Jodhpur was simply soul satisfying.

However, our life took a heart-wrenching turn when we lost our dear doggie companion, Amigo. He had been a part of our lives for nine long years and had infused us with so much joy and love. But just when we thought we would never recover from his loss, a new member joined our family in the form of Mannu Singh (a rescue Indie). Our son Jaskirat brought him home during one of his visits from Delhi (Kirat had to continue his studies in Delhi as it was not appropriate to disturb his schooling at this stage) and hid him in the guard quarters with strict instructions not to disclose this pup kidnapping and stashing away to me. Mannu quickly became an integral companion of the boys well hidden from my eyes for at least a few days. As they say, all secrets, no matter how well-kept, spill out when the time is ripe. I was sitting on the front porch of my house when this little joyful fellow came jumping and sat next to me. With his energetic personality and spiky collar, he won us over and helped us to ease the pain of Amigo's moving on to the doggy heavens.

Although Mannu has been a terrific addition to our family, we still miss Amigo and fondly remember all the happiness he brought into our lives. It's a reminder of the preciousness of life and the impact that our pets can have on our hearts.

Upon arriving in Jodhpur, we were given the privilege of residing in a beautiful appointment bungalow. Behold friends, with this new role came along. We were provided with comfort and support so that we could focus on shouldering our significant duties. In Sheri's case, it meant taking care of not just one, but many regiments.

Being a spouse, I suddenly found myself responsible for the well-being of not only young ladies, but also the task of overseeing the needs of over a thousand soldier families. It was clear that handling this required a strong team effort. I had to motivate not just the younger ladies, but also the ones senior to me in age and experience.

Balancing work, home, and taking care of Kirat during his demanding years in senior school was a daunting task. With my husband's responsibilities increasing manifolds, made our life extremely busy and filled with learning opportunities. We were assigned to run a small shop of essentials for our troops and their families, and my previous experience with Fabindia came in handy. Customer service and experience were our priorities, and soon, the shop became incredibly popular within our campus. The word spread everywhere. It became an essential stopover for any lady passing through the station, and the shopping experience was worth it. When spouses complain, they had to pay for excess baggage on return.

Despite the busyness which kept us on our toes, we made sure to take breaks and explore the surrounding areas, including a short trip to Jaisalmer, Udaipur, Mt Abu, Kutch, and Ahmedabad. I was lucky to have a group of close girlfriends, Lyla, Tannu, Dolly, Preet, Neeru, Sharmishta, Kavita and

Joseline, who made our time in Jodhpur even more interesting and filled with laughter. The shopping escapades to the old city interiors, explorations to the nearby step-well café and the enriching experience of the furniture markets made a significant hole in our bank balance, for we indulged in a few exotic timeless pieces. Till date, the Jharokha (Large window or the walkway with a fitted-glass) acts as a perfect photograph backdrop in our humble abode.

But our involvement didn't stop there. We took immense pride in our contribution and expertise in caring for a small kindergarten for the station's families, and the school for the senior children. The Army school fell under our umbrella too. With changing times, the education system is now focusing on introducing inclusive education, so an attempt to create an inclusive education room to help children facing challenges in subjects like STEM and languages was set up. An operational room with all the necessary equipment and inviting interiors was created to support children with learning disabilities. This pilot project was well-received, and we organised a large-scale program to identify and assist children from kindergarten to eighth grade over six months.

During this time, we were also entrusted with the task of creating a sensory park for the children of the station. With unimaginable dedication, the park materialised into a state-of-the-art, enriching space for generations to come.

These experiences were both extremely challenging and rewarding. They taught me the importance of teamwork, adaptability, and making a positive impact on the lives of others. It was a fulfilling journey where we strived to serve our community and contribute to a better future for our children.

During one of our wild escapades to visit a battalion, fate played a little prank on me—a rib-tickling incident that left me scrambling at the last minute. I'm told, with barely a moment's notice, to gear up for six-hour journey spanning two days. So, like a tornado on a mission, I threw my formal clothes into my bag faster than you can say "attention! "Now, the military wisdom that's been ingrained in me had a failsafe mantra for wardrobe dilemmas: when in doubt, wear a Sari— our national dress for women. Armed with this foolproof advice, I was ready to conquer the world (or at least a battalion visit).

Loaded up in our official vehicle, we embarked on our adventure. But lo-and-behold, as we unpacked our bags upon arrival, disaster struck—my precious stilettoes were nowhere to be found! Cue horror movie scream. How did we manage to overcome such a crucial accessory? It was a fashion emergency, and I needed a hero.

In my moment of distress, I speed-dialled the local "COW," Anupam, and spilled my heart out. Now, let me tell you, Anupam is no ordinary woman—she's a magician in disguise. Her response was as swift as a military operation: "Don't worry, Mrs Panjrath! "In a mere 10 minutes, I found myself facing an array of footwear, fit for a fashionista's dreams. Six pairs, to be precise, ranging from size five to eight. It was a Cinderella moment, minus the fairy godmother and the pumpkin carriage.

Now, armed with my newfound treasures, I strutted into dinner that evening. With all the grace and poise, I could muster, I raised my glass and made a grand announcement. "Ladies and gentlemen," I declared, "I want to extend my heartfelt gratitude to Cinderella, who, in a moment of sheer compassion, rescued me from the depths of footwear despair. Bless her kind *"soles"* and that, my friends, is how a visit turned into a tale of fashion heroism and the magic of military camaraderie.

Our sojourn in Jodhpur was graced by two remarkable milestones that remain etched in our hearts. First, amidst the enchanting allure of the city's landscapes, we joyously celebrated our silver anniversary, a testament to twenty-five years brimming with love and companionship. Second, the grandeur of Jodhpur served as a splendid backdrop for Sheri's 50th birthday, a milestone we embraced with panache and delight. Jodhpur's rustic charm, coupled with its iconic forts that stood as sentinels over the town, provided an ideal setting for these cherished occasions. The city's cultural richness and vibrant ambience accentuated the significance of our festivities, ensuring that the memories would endure.

Our time in Jodhpur was adorned with memorable visits to the majestic Mehrangarh Fort. We were esteemed guests during Maharaja Gaj Singh Ji's birthday celebrations at the resplendent Umaid Palace. The rooftop restaurants nestled within historic havelis offered a culinary extravaganza, where we relished local flavours while feasting our eyes on panoramic vistas.

As a military community, we were humbled by the city's admiration. The echoes of history reverberated through the polo matches organised by the local authorities, a tribute to tradition and sportsmanship that resonated with Jodhpur's heritage. We were an integral part of this regal event every year and didn't miss it for anything. The annual Rajasthan Local Folk Festival at Mehrangarh Fort was a vibrant ode to the region's cultural legacy, filling the air with captivating melodies and dance.

Among the many enchanting experiences, the Blue City Walk stands out—a captivating journey through vibrant alleys that culminated in the simple joy of a kachori and tea stall. This exploration allowed us to immerse ourselves in the local way of life, forging connections and memories that lingered beyond our departure.

Jodhpur, with its warm embrace and diverse offerings, has carved a special niche in our hearts. As we reminisce about those moments, we do so with fondness and gratitude, recognising the profound impact of varied cultures and environments on the tapestry of our lives.

Assuming the role of a senior spouse entailed a multifaceted journey, primarily focused on offering guidance and unwavering support to the spouses of Commanding Officers, who numbered five. Having traversed a similar juncture, one could empathise with the compelling responsibilities and commitments that came with the position.

In this realm, one exercised caution not to intrude into the unique customs and established ethos of each regiment, recognizing the need for individuals to assume their designated responsibilities. Instead, the objective was to stand as a robust support system for these spouses. All regiments boasted distinctive traditions and operating environments, requiring each to shoulder their designated responsibilities with utmost dedication.

At higher echelons, assuming this role appeared seamless, thanks to the camaraderie fostered by seasoned seniors who offered invaluable guidance at every step. Contrary to the notion that learning never ceased, this role served as an intermediary, continuously presenting fresh opportunities for growth and understanding. Undoubtedly, this position was not only pivotal but also wielded considerable influence in fostering a supportive community.

Flying Solo: The Evolution of Empty Nesters – 2019

A s our son Jaskirat was growing up and reaching the ripe age of 18, it was time for him to take on the world. With his dreams and ambitions beginning to get sorted, he finished his twelfth grade and was now ready to move on to college.

As a parent, it was a bittersweet moment for me to see my son, Jaskirat, growing up and embarking on a new journey to college. He had been accepted into the prestigious Parsons School of Design in New York City, but unfortunately, Sheri's visa approval came too late for him to join us on this exciting adventure. So, Jaskirat and I left for San Francisco to spend some time with Rohini, Miguel, and their children, I remember the anticipation and nervousness I felt as we walked towards their doorstep, eager to see the children that we had known so long ago. It was heartwarming to see that despite the years that had passed, our bond as a family had remained intact.

Kirat and I then headed to Baltimore, our next stop. It was to visit Lily and Cyrus and their children. Lily was Sheri's childhood friend whom we had last met in Mumbai when Kirat was born. They are to us a part of our extended family. It had been 18 long years since we had seen them, and I was eager to rekindle our bond.

The week at Baltimore passed by quickly, and before we knew it, it was time for Jaskirat to officially start his college journey. Leaving him in a new city, in a foreign land, was not easy, but I knew he was ready for this new chapter in his life. Just like the migratory birds, he was embarking on his own journey to new horizons and exploring uncharted territories. I couldn't be prouder of the young man he had become.

As I stepped out of the cab and onto the bustling streets of New York, I couldn't help but feel a mix of excitement and nervousness. The city was awake and alive at the early hour of our arrival, and I couldn't help but feel a sense of wonder as I took it all in. Kirat was eager to start his new journey at the Parsons School of Design and I was excited for him, but also a little apprehensive about the change.

It was a bittersweet feeling for Sheri and me as we went through this transitional phase of our lives. Kirat would soon adjust to life at the Parsons School of Design in New York, in a foreign land on a different continent. It was sure to be a substantial change for him, but we were confident that he would be able to thrive in his new environment.

As parents, we all go through this phase in our lives, and it can be a rollercoaster of emotions. But we were excited for Kirat and all the new experiences that awaited him in the city that never sleeps. From the bustling streets of New York to the lights of Times Square, Kirat was now a part of the hustle and bustle of one of the most exciting cities in the world.

New York was alive and buzzing with activity that early morning when we hopped off at Penn Station. Eager to explore the city, we hailed a taxi and rushed to our hotel. Kirat couldn't wait to start his college journey and take charge of his life. His excitement was infectious! To add to the excitement, it started to rain. But rain in New York is no ordinary rain - it's a whole production! Fire tenders and NYPD were everywhere, to make sure the raindrops didn't misbehave. Talk about overwhelming hospitality!

And speaking of misbehaving, Google played a little prank on us. It led us to the wrong hotel, and we wandered the streets like lost souls with our four bags and two suitcases (our adorable stuffed toys, mind you). Imagine our relief when we finally found the right place! To our surprise, the hotel room turned out to be smaller than we expected. It was like one of those comical scenes from a movie, where you open the door, and the room is gone! But we made the most of it and called it an adventure.

The college was situated inside a typical skyscraper. The building had classes on the ground levels and dorms on the higher levels. They had allocated Kirat a suite with five roommates, situated right above the classes. The thought of living in a high-rise was both thrilling and intimidating for him. But hey, it's New York, and everything here is bound to be larger than life!

The next day was all about parents' orientations, and boy, were we involved in various activities! It was like running a marathon from one end of the block to the other. We were taken on a campus tour, which was supposed to make us familiar with the surroundings, but instead, we were just left panting and sweating. Who knew orientation could be such a workout?

In the end, the parents' orientations were a rollercoaster of emotions, from exhaustion to laughter. New York welcomed us with open arms, and we were ready to absorb every moment of this thrilling chapter in Kirat's life. Who knew that navigating through this concrete jungle would be so much fun, challenging, and rewarding all at once?

As Kirat started his college journey and I bid farewell to our little boy turned New York adventurer, we knew this city had already stolen a piece of our hearts. And with that, the New York chapter began, with adjustments, the rain, lost ways, cramped rooms, snow blizzards and a lot of love and laughter!

With a sense of pride and excitement, I watched Kirat as he commenced his new life in New York, taking advantage of all the opportunities that were available to him. It was a thrilling journey that would shape him as a better person and human being.

As a proud mother, I took advantage of my time in New York to immerse myself in the city's rich culture and history. Being there during Parents' Orientation, I made sure to take every opportunity to explore the city, as it was a once-in-a-lifetime experience. I took a stunning ferry ride along the Hudson River, soaking in the city's beauty from the water. I also took a night trip to New York's iconic Times Square, the Statue of Liberty, and the Flatron Building, which was simply awe-inspiring. One of the highlights of my trip was shopping, of course! I discovered the city's bustling shopping districts, with high-end retailers like Macy's, Zara, JC Penny, and Marshalls. It's true what they say: shopping is the best therapy for a woman, and I was more than happy to indulge in some retail therapy during my time in New York.

As much as I was having a blast, my son Kirat was more than content to make new friends and get settled in at his dorm. I could tell that he was eager to take on the responsibilities of college life and chart his own course. It was heartwarming to see him growing into an independent young man, and I was grateful to have been there to witness it all.

As I boarded my return flight from New York to India, I couldn't help but feel a pang of sadness in my heart. It was the fourth day after the Sophomore Walk, and it was time to leave Jaskirat, behind in this bustling city. Leaving your child miles away in an unknown land is never easy, he is your only child. Friends and family tried to console me by saying things like "It's just a phase" and "he's going to have the time of his life," but I couldn't shake off the feeling of loneliness.

As I sat on the plane, I reminisced about the final day on the campus of the Parsons School of Design. Jaskirat had called me back and said, "You can hug me tight, Mummy." I hugged him tightly and didn't turn back, even though my eyes were filled with tears. The journey back to the airport was the longest and loneliest I had ever experienced. I was now officially an "empty nester."

But I reminded myself that this was exactly what Jaskirat needed at this stage of his life. He was about to embark on a journey filled with new experiences, from making connections and forming new relationships to encountering both the highs and lows of life. I was confident that the skills and lessons he would learn in the coming years would help him mature into a confident and well-rounded adult.

It's like the saying goes, "empty nest is just a temporary goodbye before the reunion of a lifetime." And I couldn't wait for that day to come. But until then, I knew I had to let Jaskirat spread his wings and fly.

At that time, I didn't know how I would feel or even manage my time. I was always the helicopter mom. His schedule had kept me busy, and I learned to enjoy every moment...and then it stopped! Not suddenly, since I knew, he was leaving to go away to college, but it felt abrupt enough to leave me unsure of what to do with my time. Letting go was a challenge.

Fast forward to this day; I am happy that I have adjusted although I do realise that there are many benefits to being an empty nester.

Discovering My Real Self

This time as an empty nester has been filled with many moments of me getting to know myself. I was 27 when our first and only child was born; I fell in love with being a mom. Motherhood is a true blessing, and I am proud to have been able to nurture, protect, and be there for him. But as I sat alone for the first time not having to cook, or run to a call from the school, I realised I didn't know myself. This initial discovery was overwhelming and scary. Thinking more about me was a concept that I had to now get accustomed to.

Being purposeful in all that I do has become a priority. I have learned to say no and focus on doing what brings me joy. My health and peace are vital, and my mindset is "Why Not Me?" I am more than a mom. Why not me as an entrepreneur, motivational speaker, or world traveller? Taking the time to understand and embrace my interests has been an exciting venture. The list is endless, and I am still trying to enjoy discovering myself.

Rekindling My Relationships

The empty-nesting period has allowed time for me to reconnect with my husband. I must admit, it wasn't easy at first. It was a struggle to figure out who we were as a couple and what we still had in common. Taking the time to communicate our individual needs has become a priority. Fewer demands on me have allowed more time and opportunities for an emotional connection. Reigniting our partnership and creating meaningful connections without our son has improved the quality of our relationship.

Acquainting myself with friends around me, rekindling long-lost friendships, and giving guilt-free time to the organisation that gave me my wings are a few things I choose to pursue today.

Appreciating Peace and Quiet

The absence of teenager arguing over food, TV time, computers, unfinished tiffins and even missing school bus is a welcome change. There are days when I can hear a pin drop. I never fully understood that this type of quietness existed. On the nights that I am completely alone in the house, I look forward to eating in bed and watching Netflix or making reels on Instagram. The serenity is intoxicating, a feeling that creates a sense of peace. I have learned to fully embrace this as self-care, as a time for myself that is much needed to centre my peace and to embrace the moment.

No one can truly prepare you for what happens when your children turn eighteen and leave the nest. They are not "leaving" but going out into the world to experience a life in which we have prepared them to flourish. I force myself to think I have done my job well. My child is independent, capable, adventurous, everything that I could have dreamed of and more.

This is a new chapter in my life, and "I must trust the process and embrace the progress."

Time to Recollect and Reminisce – 2020-2022

The year 2020 was a rollercoaster ride for the entire world, and it was no different for me. I was in the middle of a journey, with hundreds of people from various countries, including Brazil and Australia, when the Pandemic hit. Sudden news of the pandemic spread like wildfire. During this time, no one knew what the impact would be. We didn't even know what was going to happen or how long this uncertainty would last. The flights had been grounded and there was uncertainty in the air. While the world was contemplating measures to be taken, my son Kirat was visiting his Aunt Lily in Baltimore, during the thanksgiving break from his college. Lily was Sheri's childhood friend whom we had spoken about earlier in the Mumbai episode. She and her family lived in Baltimore, about four hours away from New York. She had been instrumental in guiding us initially when Kirat was about to be born and now when Kirat was an undergraduate student. It was at her place when he got to know that the college had shut down its dorms.

Lily, being the amazing friend she was, kept Kirat safe with her for three months, or even more. Along with Kirat and her two children, she took on the responsibility of another friend's daughter, too. It was informed by the college to its students that they would ascertain the situation after two months and decide if students could come back to New York. The college gave a three-hour window for students to clear their dorm rooms and take away their belongings. I am being, the Helicopter parent sprang into action. I reached out to the parents' group to find a place to store Kirat's belongings, and that's when I received a message from a lady named Gwen. Gwen was the spouse of one of the Directors of the college and stayed in Pennsylvania. Her son Nathaniel, a sophomore, also attended the same college as Kirat, and she offered to keep all his belongings in her home until he returned.

I asked Gwen to let her son Nathaneil wait for Kirat to reach New York and pack his belongings, but she had a better plan in place. She told me that her son would take the train from Pennsylvania and help Kirat pack everything up. The kindness of strangers never ceases to amaze me, and Gwen's gesture was an authentic example of this. It made me smile amid a chaotic situation and gave me some comfort in knowing that there were still good people out there. On the designated day, Jaskirat reached the Dorm at sharp 12 PM. To his surprise, Nathaniel was there. As he packed his belongings, his passport was nowhere to be found. It was the most terrifying news for us as parents. I was praying aloud, possibly read all the "Sarv Dharm "all prayers in all religions I knew, prancing around, just as my mother used to. Amidst this panic, my husband decided he would retire for the day. Precisely at ten minutes to three, Kirat found his passport stuck in between the writing table and the wall. We heaved a sigh of relief. The boys shifted everything into Nathaniels' dorm room and went to catch their train and head back.

God truly does work in mysterious ways, and Gwen and her family were a shining example of that. They had entered our lives just at the right moment when the world was plunged into uncertainty and chaos due to the pandemic. Travel restrictions made it difficult for Kirat to return and retrieve his belongings, but Gwen stepped up to the plate and offered to keep his things safe until he was able to return. Her generosity was a beacon of hope in a dark time, and I will always be grateful to her for that.

Jaskirat, my son, was a rising senior in college, growing and learning with each passing day, facing the challenges of young adulthood with determination and resilience. He told me that the journey had helped him "take on his own," which fills me with pride and joy as a mother. And when Kirat was finally able to return to India on the last Vande Bharat flight, our happiness knew no boundaries. He was with us for eight months in India. It was a difficult period for him considering the time zones, which hampered his sleep patterns, practically attending classes all night. Finally, after eight months, the college announced the start of hybrid classes. Sheri was wary of the second wave hitting India. He suggested putting Kirat on the flight back as soon as possible. The flight of his return was booked on British Airways who informed us on the last day that there was just no possibility of Kirat boarding the flight as he was an Indian national and only US passport holders were permitted for a transit. Sheri, the cool father amidst all this chaos, went to the airport and called us to reach the airport after an hour.

One could imagine Kirat, me all running around, packing his computer and belongings and rushing off to the departures of T3 international airport Delhi. Sheri had managed to get a direct flight to New York at half the cost. Upon reaching New York, Kirat parked himself at a friend's place. By the end of the week, he quarantined himself, put inoculations, and had started apartment hunting along with attending classes. Kirat found an apartment in Brooklyn and moved in with a roommate. Craig and Nathaniel, Gwen's husband and son, went out of their way to personally deliver Kirat's belongings to him. This act of kindness, in a world that can often feel harsh and unforgiving, reminds me of the beauty and compassion that still exists in humanity.

Time has been a funny concept lately, hasn't it? It seems like only yesterday we were sending our son Kirat off to college in the United States, and now, suddenly, two years have flown by in the blink of an eye. Yet so much happened in those two years. It's almost like we've lived a lifetime in just two short years.

Looking back, I am grateful for the opportunities and experiences we've had, the lessons we've learned, and the new relationships we've formed. It's a reminder that even in the darkest of times, there is always a light at the end of the tunnel and that there is always someone out there who is willing to lend a helping hand. I am filled with gratitude for Gwen and her family, who went beyond to help us during a time of uncertainty, and I will always be thankful for the kindness and compassion they showed us.

So, here's to timing, and all the adventures, both big and small, that it brings our way. Here's to learning and growing, and to never taking a single moment for granted. Time flew by. Kirat went on to his third year in college. By now, he had an internship. He knew the place well and had made friends. As parents, we have a strong inclination when our children are homesick. My father-in-law had gone to visit my sister-in-law in Jan 2020 when the pandemic struck. Being a senior citizen, we didn't want him to travel during covid, so he stayed back with her family in San Francisco. It had been over two years for him. So, I planned to visit him and Kirat (who by now had moved to an apartment in Jersey City) in June 2022. I landed on the 9th of June 2022, early rainy morning at the alluring JFK airport.

As I sat at my son Kirat's writing table in the bustling city of Jersey, I reflected on the 49 years and 8 months that had gone by. Kirat was here in the city, working hard on a summer internship, and it had been a blissful six months since he had been away from us. However, if it weren't for his return home during the summers, I would have gone an entire year without seeing him.

Some may question a mother's visit to her son in college, but I couldn't resist the opportunity to see him. The moment I arrived, a series of questions came my way, ranging from "Why did you come?" to "When are you leaving?" and even "I can manage on my own!" I could hear the frustration in my son's voice, but I was determined to stay and be there for him.

In many cultures around the world, it is common for mothers to visit their children, even in college. It's a testament to the strong bond between a mother and her child. I know my visit may have disrupted his summer plans, but I believe that a mother's love knows no bounds. I'm ready to weather any storm and make the most of my time here with Kirat.

Moving from Brooklyn to Jersey City was not Jaskirat's first choice, but it turned out to be a blessing in disguise. The stay in Brooklyn for Kirat had been a little disappointing in terms of the landlord mafia. Skyrocketing rentals and making a mockery of international students. But he had his lifeline there, his family and his friends. As parents, we had to force him to move out from Brooklyn to New Jersey, where the scene was more comfortable to handle for us being so far away. Brooklyn couldn't have been matched for starters, we had access to all the comfort food we could ever want, a spacious and clean-living space, and a shorter commute to work, not to mention the Gurudwara, our religious place was just a stone's throw away. I took it upon myself to prepare two delicious meals for us each day, with Kirat's lunch being provided by his office. And of course, I always look forward to welcoming him back home each day.

We realised that as international students; it was evident that we had to keep a roommate who would share his rental. We quickly put our apartment on rental platforms and our new roommate was soon about to move in, and everything was gradually falling into place. It's amazing how sometimes a change of scene can lead to new and unexpected experiences.

We often compare our experiences with those of others, such as a young student in Paris who might be having croissants for breakfast and exploring the city's iconic landmarks. Or a family in India who might be enjoying butter chicken for dinner and navigating the busy streets of the city's vibrant neighbourhoods.

It's interesting to see how different cultures and lifestyles shape our experiences, but at the end of the day, what matters most is being together and creating memories that will last a lifetime. Whether it's in Brooklyn, Jersey City, or anywhere else in the world, the love and support of family always prevails.

As a parent, it's only natural to feel fractionally apprehensive about moving to a new place, especially when it is with your grown-up child who has a life of their own. But let me tell you, sometimes change can be the best thing that ever happened to you. Just like how they say, "When one door closes, another opens." I had persuaded my son Kirat to move from Brooklyn to Jersey City, and despite his initial reluctance, he would eventually see the positive side of the move.

While in Jersey, we took a trip to Texas to visit my cousin Dolly (whom we had discussed about in my childhood chapters) and her family. It was a treat to watch the cousin's bond, Kirat and Samaira, her daughter, hitting it off right away. My cousin's husband, Sumeet, made sure that Kirat had the time of his life. He took us on a tour of Austin (an intriguing town filled with the design community) and San Antonio, the place with rich history and the vibes of a mini-Venice. I haven't seen Kirat enjoy himself this much since he joined college. Especially when in the water park he went on a water roller coaster and the giant wheel for the second time.

And as they say, everything happens for a reason. This trip was just what Kirat needed to rekindle his love for adventure and travel. It was also a pleasant reminder for me to cherish every moment and to never take for granted the joys of spending time with our loved ones. So, here's to new beginnings and fresh adventures! Kirat's college began that week and he became a senior.

I travelled back to India on the 9th of September 2022.

At Home in India, We Entered 'Raksha Bhawan' - The Abode of Lifelong Friendship!!

Rajasthan sojourn brought us towards an important milestone in Sheri's career. He had been nominated for the NDC. For the spouse's point of perspective, the first question on hearing he had been nominated for the prestigious 60th National Defence College course was, "So, do we get to stay in the legendary Raksha Bhawan?" I mean, come on, it's practically the Big Daddy of all officer accommodations! The excitement mixed with nerves was like waiting for exam results, promotion news, and the next season of your favourite show all rolled into one. Let me tell you this, the mother of all the courses we have done so far. Again, a reminder that we could go back to being stress free and get a few moments of being ourselves, without the need to be on guard.

So, for all you novices' friends out there, Raksha Bhawan isn't just a place to crash during the course. It's like a swanky officers' utopia where the Army, Air Force, Navy, civil services, and international officers from around the globe gather to live under one roof. Imagine the United Nations, but with more epaulets and fewer PowerPoint presentations.

Visually, Raksha Bhawan might look like a series of eccentric, mismatched double-storied bungalows stacked like Tetris pieces. But don't be fooled – this is where the real deal happens! Each block of twelve houses comes with its own little backyard garden, which, during the pandemic lockdown, became our oasis. Move over, Netflix – those backyard hangouts were our binge-worthy salvation during those dicey pandemic times.

Now, I resided in Block B, which felt like its own sitcom set. Picture this: officers analysing the finer points of their surroundings, holding serious discussions about the strategic placement of baby watermelons and lemon trees. You could practically hear the bungalows gossiping about it all night. Life at Raksha Bhawan wasn't just a routine; it was a rollercoaster of quirkiness and camaraderie.

Speaking of camaraderie, imagine cramming forty families onto one campus during a pandemic. We were like a close-knit mini city, more of a social experiment than a course. Rainstorms? Impromptu tea parties happened. First instance of getting a little happy? Let's just say some senior officers discovered their inner youthful cadet once again, much to everyone's amusement. And those empty nesters who suddenly had their fledglings back home during the COVID chaos? Well, let's just say the nest was suddenly more crowded than a subway during rush hour. One month into the course and we had the pandemic striking globally. This didn't dampen our morale because we all were in this together. The regular classes went online for the officers. Ladies were confined to the kitchen and looking after families.

Ah, but we were well cared for. Our very own coursemate and campus doctor became our very own superhero, made sure we were more vigilant about our health than an eagle eyeing its prey. Thanks to his watchful guidance, we sailed through the year without so much as a sniffle.

Post six months into the pandemic, me and Sheri took the courage to wish our neighbours and friends on their anniversaries, still unsure it took great courage to do it in person. The hosts had a spread of wine waiting for their guests. I took the liberty to indulge. What followed was a disaster that went home with me. But post this incident, bubbles of interactions started happening and finally the whole Raksha Bhawan was in party mode. Even our overseas friends who were alone and locked up in their rooms came out to celebrate friendship.

And talking about celebrations? Oh boy, Raksha Bhawan knew how to throw a party. From Indian festivities (Lohri, Holi, Eid, Garbha, Karvachauth and even Diwali) that could rival a Bollywood movie set to international events that showcased a pot-pourri of cultures, we were the Masters of Ceremonies in the art of revelry.

Sure, our overseas trips might've been cancelled, but who needed them? We were too busy forging bonds that went beyond borders. We became a family of brothers and sisters in arms, facing the challenges of the world head-on while creating memories that even the best holiday couldn't match.

So, there you have it – Raksha Bhawan, not just a residence but a vibrant tapestry of tales, triumphs, and the occasional misplaced watermelon debate. Here's to the 60th NDC course and the legendary saga that unfolded within those quirky walls!

While the course ended after eleven months' duration, the bonds created during the pandemic times became thicker. Many of our colleagues flew back to their countries or places of assignment. Few of us got posted to Delhi and continued our professional journey from here.

One individual from our course who truly stands out in my memory is Brigadier Lakhwinder Singh Lidder. Even after our course at the National Defence College concluded, he remained connected with us as he took up a posting in Delhi. His role as the Military Assistant to the Chief of Defence Staff, General Rawat. His vibrant personality had earned him the affectionate nickname "Toni" from all who knew him. Toni brought an unparalleled vibrancy to our course at the NDC. No gathering or celebration was complete without his larger-than-life presence. He had a remarkable ability to spread joy and laughter wherever he went. His hearty voice would always reach out to me with a genial "Gonu Maam," creating an instant connection that exemplified his warm nature.

Toni passionately believed in embracing life to its fullest extent and consistently encouraged all of us to do the same. His mantra, *"Hum to retirement friends hain"* - signifying that our friendships would continue beyond retirement - resonated deeply with us. In essence, we had become an extended family of his own, bound together by shared experiences and a shared outlook on life. This natural bond was a testament to the concept of "retirement friends," something that our upbringing had instilled within us.

Toni's sudden absence served as a poignant reminder that life can change in the blink of an eye. It reinforced the values of empathy and human compassion that were an integral part of our collective upbringing. His legacy lives on in the powerful lesson he imparted: to seize life's moments with gusto, to focus on quality rather than quantity, and to cherish the connections that make us a family, regardless of the circumstances.

With time, we became an extended family to his own, as indeed we were retirement friends. This dynamic evolved organically, guided by our shared experiences and values. In a poignant twist of fate, Toni's abrupt departure underlined the unpredictability of life.

The journey after this extreme incident crawled to its own pace. With heavy hearts, we bid adieu and gathered our courage and strength to go ahead. It's interesting to understand sometimes the motivation and support is right beside us all the time. Armed forces are invisible joint families beside their martyrs. Families of the fallen comrades become an integral part of army fraternity for life.

As I reach the milestone of fifty years, I reflect on my journey with a sense of gratitude and fulfilment. I have had the opportunity to experience life in all its hues and colours and have had some incredible experiences that I will cherish forever. I am grateful for the lessons I have learned, the people I have met, and the memories I have created. As I look back at my fifty-year journey, I realise how rich and fulfilling it has been. I have had the privilege of meeting and interacting with some of the most incredible individuals who have touched my life in ways that I could have never imagined. Some of these individuals have become an integral part of my life, while others are cherished memories that will remain etched in my heart forever.

Looking ahead, I am excited about what the future holds. My journey has just begun, and I am eager to see where it takes me next. I am confident that no matter what life brings, I will continue to live it to the fullest, just like our loved ones encouraged us all to do.

As a child of an army officer, I was raised in a world where discipline, trust, and resilience were at the forefront of every decision. I learned the importance of hard work and dedication, as I saw my father serve our country with pride. I was witness to the sadness that comes with transfers, as we said goodbye to friends and the familiar comforts of one station, only to start anew in another. But the army is more than just a job, it's a way of life. The sense of camaraderie and love that I have experienced as a military spouse is something that I will cherish forever.

My journey as a military spouse has taught me the value of discipline, trust, resilience, and hard work. I have experienced the difficulties of life in the army and have formed deep bonds with those who share a similar path. But most importantly, I have learned that no matter where life takes me; it is the people I am surrounded by that make it a journey worth taking. The memories of my transition in the army are vast and varied, but they all come back to one central theme: the power of community. Whether it was in the form of close friends, fellow military spouses, or simply the knowledge that I was part of something larger than myself, I was never truly alone.

I have had the privilege of serving alongside my husband, as a senior officer's wife, and I have seen first-hand the confidence and unwavering commitment with which our military members serve our country. Through all the challenges that come with being part of the army family, I have learned to trust in the strength and resilience of those around me.

Epilude:
Army Life "Roles &
Reflections"

And there you have it, the whirlwind journey of a girl who grew up under the watchful eye of camouflage nets, marched alongside her partner in both love and service, and now finds herself as a seasoned guide for the next generation of army spouses. If life were a play, I'd say I've been cast in some of its most challenging yet rewarding roles – the resilient army child, the steadfast army spouse, and now, the sage senior lady spouse.

As I reflect upon the pages of my life, it's hard not to chuckle at the thought of how far we've come from the days of my father's trusty Bajaj scooter to cruising around in our modern-day MG Hector. I'm tempted to wonder if my dear old scooter would've even recognised the luxury on four wheels that we zip around in today!

But let's not get too carried away – after all, humility is a virtue we've held close to our hearts in this journey. And speaking of humility, let's not forget the endless hours I spent perfecting the art of setting up a new home at the speed of light. Yes, relocating was our version of "Extreme Makeover: Home Edition," with a dash of military precision. The moment we got the call for a new posting, it was a whirlwind of packing, unpacking, and figuring out which box contained the four-burner gas stove — the real MVP of those trying times.

And let's talk about camaraderie – the lifeline of the military spouse. If only I had a rupee for every time a fellow spouse lent an understanding ear or a shoulder to cry on during those long deployments. We might not have always been in the same unit, but we were certainly in the same army of fortitude, resilience, and a shared love for complaining about the scarcity of decent housing.

To the uninitiated reader, I hope my story has cracked open the camouflage door to reveal the everyday lives of those who stand steadfastly behind the uniforms. We're not just about polished boots and stoic expressions; we're a vibrant tapestry of personalities, dreams, and, dare I say, quirky quirks.

Now, if you're still a tad sceptical about the notion of an army groom sweeping you off your feet, consider this: they've been trained to handle high-pressure situations, navigate through the most perplexing terrains (both on maps and in relationships), and master the art of keeping their cool when the going gets tough. Plus, I've always believed that anyone who can handle a chaotic Mess tent during chow time is more than equipped to handle life's everyday messes.

As the curtain falls on this chapter, I look ahead with anticipation, armed with the lessons of the past and the promise of the future. There's a sparkle in my eye as I imagine the roles of a loving mother-in-law and a young-at-heart grandmother. The road ahead might be uncertain, but if my journey has taught me anything, it's that with a dose of courage, a sprinkle of laughter, and a heart full of love, there's no adventure too daunting.

So, my friends, keep your spirits high and your coffee stronger – life's journey is a rollercoaster, but you've got a front-row seat. And who knows, one day we'll trade tales of bravery and laughter over a cup of chai, as we regale the younger generation with the epic sagas of army life, where the challenges were aplenty, but so were the bonds that held us all together.

Onward, army-strong, and onward we go!

Mission Gratitude

I'm profoundly thankful for the gifted individuals who've breathed life into this book with their vibrant caricatures, illustrations, and captivating cover design. Together, their diverse talents have beautifully captured the essence of my journey. Their unwavering dedication and support have been invaluable, and my gratitude for them knows no bounds. Interestingly they all have one thing in common their service background!

1. Anshuman Chatterjee – Illustrations- Capt. Anshuman Chatterjee, Retd. (Indian Navy) is a self-taught artist who draws, paints and sketches to focus his thoughts and see the humour in everyday life. Primarily a cartoonist with a dry sense of humour he has contributed to a lot of journals and books. He can be found on twitter (@chatterjeea330) and Instagram as (@chats_cartoons)

2. Maryam Ahmad - Cover Design- Maryam Ahmad is a freelance digital and traditional artist, a children's book illustrator, 2D animator and now a Ceramic Artist. She is also an Art Educator as well as a Brand Ambassador for the paper. brand: Scholar

3. KD Singh - KD Singh is an officer in the Corp of Army Air Defence. Known by his initials KD fondly, he is a fervent caricaturist. He loves to display his zeal towards the art and emotions humorously through his digital and pencil work. His work has found recognition widely across the army in the form of Rouges Galleries at various Army Mess across various arms. He has been vehemently appreciated for his portrayal of "Humour in Uniform." His artistry ought to add that smile on the reader's faces when his created characters come to life through his drawings.

4. Riya – Internee with Creative Crows Publishers- Riya is a visual storyteller/ illustrator based in India. My work portrays emotive, meaningful, and impactful visual narratives. I am deeply inspired by the life that thrives around me which is also the reason behind being a sketchbook enthusiast.

5. Mosiur Rehman- The Editor & Designer- He is a self-taught graphic designer, an avid reader, blogger and Chief Editor at The Hyderabad Review. His passion for art and literature since childhood has made the man he is today.